CW00505743

et Shop Boys versus America. A book by Chris Heath. Photographs by Pennie Smith.

VIKING

VIKING

Published by the Penguin Group
Penguin Books Ltd, 27 Wrights Lane, London W8 5TZ, England
Penguin Books USA Inc., 375 Hudson Street, New York, New York 10014, USA
Penguin Books Australia Ltd, Ringwood, Victoria, Australia
Penguin Books Canada Ltd, 10 Alcorn Avenue, Toronto, Ontario, Canada M4V 3B2
Penguin Books (NZ) Ltd, 182–190 Wairau Road, Auckland 10, New Zealand

Penguin Books Ltd, Registered Offices: Harmondsworth, Middlesex, England

First published 1993
1 3 5 7 9 10 8 6 4 2
First edition

Copyright © Areagraph Ltd, 1993

Filmset in Monophoto Bembo by Selwood Systems, Midsomer Norton

Printed in Singapore by Kyodo Printing Co

A CIP catalogue record for this book is available from the British Library

ISBN 0–670–85274–0

Foreword

When we toured North America for the first time a couple of years ago, we anticipated some sort of confrontation between our pop values and theatrical presentation (no musicians on-stage) and traditional American rock values, audiences, critics. In fact the tour was a thrilling experience for us: the show worked, the audiences were enthusiastic, the crew worked incredibly hard to present a complicated production in venues of varying sizes – even some of the critics liked it.

Chris Heath and Pennie Smith travelled with us on the entire tour. This book is their record of it. We hope you enjoy it.

Neil Tennant, Chris Lowe
Pet Shop Boys

Introduction

As with most projects involving the Pet Shop Boys, this book started out with little formal brief, other than to be a combination of photographs and text recording their 1991 American tour as it travelled across fourteen cities in the USA and Canada. If there was a single idea behind it, it was one of what might happen when two very different cultures – that of the Pet Shop Boys and that of America – met. The choice of Pennie Smith as the tour photographer was influenced by her classic photographs of the Clash at American truckstops and there was certainly an expectation that she might photograph Neil and Chris against the wide open landscapes of mid-America, or leaning casually against gas pumps. If she didn't take those photos, it was because they were not there to be taken. Even in America the Pet Shop Boys were not, it turned out, the sort of people who spent very much time in fields or at gas stations.

What we recorded was rather more complicated. The Pet Shop Boys treat America with an uneasy mixture of priorities and prejudices. It is a country they face both with a sense of mission and with a sense of disdain. The same conundrum would restate itself time and again during the tour – what does it mean if they want success here but dislike so much of what modern America, and the modern American, is?

One solution – a rationalization that proud Englishmen abroad have used for generations – was to convince themselves that the Americans to whom the Pet Shop Boys appealed were somehow special. They were the disenchanted! The outcasts! The cheesed-off! In other words, they were precisely those Americans who saw in America from within the same faults the Pet Shop Boys saw from the outside. It was a good answer, and there was some truth in it, but it was never going to be the whole story.

The Pet Shop Boys had never toured in America before. In 1986 they planned to – tickets even went on sale in Los Angeles – but they pulled out when they realized how much money they would lose. A couple of years later, after the release of their *Introspective* album, they were persuaded by their American record company, EMI, that it would help their credibility with an American audience if they toured, and a private agreement was drawn up between EMI and the Pet Shop Boys whereby they would perform in at least twelve cities following the release of their next album. In 1991 Neil and Chris decided that, even though that agreement had been superseded, and even though they would still lose a large sum of money taking such an elaborate production around American theatres, they wished to undertake such a tour anyway. Nevertheless, the whole style of the show was based on a reaction to America. They had been told that you couldn't tour America successfully without a live drummer, advice which aggravated them: their response was to have no musicians on-stage whatsoever, and the theatrical nature of the performance followed from this decision. It was a typical example of the way they work: they would tour America but they wouldn't give an inch.

The spring of 1991 found them at a strange moment. Their latest album, *Behaviour*, had been widely proclaimed a masterpiece but had still sold less well than their previous records. Just before the tour a single, 'Being Boring', one of the songs they were most proud of, became their least successful single in the British charts for six years, a failure which they struggled to explain to themselves. These few months caught them by turns battling with and dismissing an unusual level of self-doubt. Often they would toy with the idea of stopping what they were doing – less, I felt, because they were genuinely considering disbanding than because raising the question reminded them why they wanted to be a pop group, and helped remind them which things they should do, and which they should not. These matters were thrown more keenly into focus by being in America – there is nowhere else where success is valued so highly, or where the decisions and sacrifices you make in chasing success are more nakedly apparent. Their American career started well – in 1986 'West End Girls' reached number one and was followed by a string of hit singles – but recently it had tailed off, and the effort required to reverse that had sometimes seemed unachievable. Their feelings about this would swing from hour to hour, from being annoyed that the largest nation of pop listeners were stubbornly resisting them to being arrogantly dismissive of anyone silly enough not to like them, to having the detached pride of those whose creative accomplishments are sufficient satisfaction in themselves, to being studiously determined to woo new converts, to keenly wanting not to even be seen to be trying to be liked. Part of this book is indeed about the Pet Shop Boys versus America, but in other parts America sits in the background and the true tussle is that of the Pet Shop Boys versus themselves.

★

One of the conceits of the previous Pet Shop Boys book, *Pet Shop Boys, Literally*, was that it treated a pop music tour as though it were the subject of social anthropology, and thus the text was ritualistically inclusive in its detail, and virtually no events of even the most mundane significance were omitted. Though scenes in this new book are often presented in the same detail, the overall text is not inclusive in the same way. The narration, just as the photographs, takes the form of snapshots. The reader is eavesdropping, and most of the time those speaking have forgotten they are being listened to.

In hindsight, Neil and Chris remember this tour as thrilling and fairly triumphant. Their memories may be unfairly skewed towards the happier times; this book, by contrast, is unfairly skewed towards the more difficult moments. The Pet Shop Boys are not the sort of people to say a huge amount during moments of exuberance, preferring to sip a little champagne, perhaps, and then move on. At times of boredom, irritation or crisis they are rather more garrulous. If in the text that follows they occasionally seem irrational, or inconsistent, or pompous, or nasty, remember that most of the words in this book aren't those of public statements but of private, everyday babble; words that, in more normal circumstances, would have been forgotten as soon as they were spoken.

Sunday, 17 March

Coconut Grove, Miami, a suburb of boutiques with pastel pink and green awnings. The Pet Shop Boys and entourage are staying at the Mayfair House Hotel. Everyone is booked under their own names except for Neil (C. Heston) and Chris (R. Welch). Across the road from the hotel Grove Calloways is holding a ZZ Top Hot Legs Contest. 'Men and women'. For the finest legs, free ZZ Top concert tickets.

On the first night in America Chris and Neil host a tour party barbecue on the hotel roof. It looks like the party scene in *Spinal Tap*, someone says. Spirits are high. They talk about Japan: amusing mishaps, the return of their number-one fan Eko, Mr Udo, the promoter they had duelled with on their last tour there. He apparently praised the show, but didn't come to see it. He threw them a party, but didn't turn up. I have just flown in. Joining a tour after it has begun is like arriving late at a party: you feel that everyone has drunk more than you and is talking about something they understand but which you yourself can't quite grasp.

In Japan they went to see one of George Michael's cover version concerts.

'We were asked backstage beforehand,' said Neil, 'and Chris made a remark about his haircut.'

'I said I really liked "Careless Whisper",' says Chris. 'And I asked, "You do 'Killer'?" and he said, "I'll do it first so you can go." '

'He always puts himself down,' says Neil. 'He tells you it's half-empty.'

Chris scowls when he is told that their new British single, 'Where the Streets Have No Name (I Can't Take My Eyes off You)', which melds a U2 song and an old Frankie Valli tune into a high-energy stomper, has entered the charts at number seven. The mid-week prediction had been number three. That afternoon Neil has been to see the film everyone is talking about, *The Doors*. No good. He says he saw it so that he would have something to talk about in interviews.

Record Mirror, *16 March, 'Strange Behaviour', an interview with Tim Nicholson:*
'This tour is going to be even more theatrical than the last one,' explains Neil. 'The last

tour was more of a theatrical event, whereas this is more operatic. There won't be any musicians onstage, just dancers and backing singers, and the songs link together lyrically. I guess the only comparison I can think of would be with David Bowie's "Diamond Dogs" tour, but even then he had some guitarist playing solos onstage.'

Won't that stick in the throats of an American audience in particular?

'Yes,' says Chris, a self-satisfied grin on his face . . .

'We've always been told,' says Neil, 'that to break really big in America you've got to tour extensively. Well, this is our response to that opinion. We're saying, "OK, we'll tour, but it will have to be on our own terms and you will have to deal with that." This tour will be a challenge to an American audience in particular because it is so alien to what they have been used to.'

Monday, 18 March

Interviews. Chris is on the phone to Dublin radio. Ticket sales for Dublin are terrible. Before he dials they wonder whether the Irish have reacted badly to their U2 cover. 'We have got a nerve,' sniggers Chris, 'doing a cover version and then slagging off the group . . .' A few minutes later he is telling the DJ he's a big U2 fan.

The next interviewer is here in person. Sasha from Paris *Elle*. There are a load of European journalists in town, flown in by EMI to see their high-priority new signing, Huey Lewis and the News. Pet Shop Boys have reluctantly agreed to see them. Sasha asks questions; Chris fiddles with his hair, uninterested, while Neil goes into a well-rehearsed spiel.

'. . . I'm not a huge opera fan. What I'm a fan of – one of the biggest things in the theatre in London is the English National Opera, because they reinterpret classic opera in very different, inventive ways. And it's also out of the rock format . . . This time we wanted to be as brave as possible. Someone told us, "When you tour America you have to have a live drummer." That's when we decided to have no musicians on-stage.'

How are the audiences reacting? Sasha asks.

'They leave halfway through,' says Chris. Then he says that actually they love it.

'I think people in the music business underestimate people,' says Neil. 'If you do things differently and with a lot of effort, they appreciate it.'

More questions.

'It's no accident,' says Neil, 'that when we do a show it's an ensemble show. We're two of fifteen people. It's not a star show.'

Do you feel more comfortable, Sasha wonders, in the studio or on-stage?

'I think when you're in the studio,' says Chris, 'you're looking forward to being on-stage, and vice versa.'

'I'm always surprised how much I like being on-stage,' says Neil.

As usual they're quizzed about their collaborations with Liza Minnelli, Dusty Springfield. Old stars, summarizes Sasha, making a comeback.

'I think we've done our bit,' says Chris.

'We haven't viewed it as helping them out,' points out Neil, worrying that the interviewer's assumption has remained unchallenged. 'We worked with them because we admire them.' But no more. 'We don't want to be categorized. The next would be someone young. I don't think there are enough young pop stars. There are too many like me who are thirty-six.'

They're asked about sampling.

'I think it's really good. It's great,' says Chris. 'I like anything that's new.'

What would you think if someone had a hit by sampling one of your records?

'I'd be thrilled to bits.' Pause. 'I'd want money off it, of course.'

Sasha leaves.

'It's not fair we have to do interviews and the band don't,' grumps Chris.

Neil doesn't respond. He is leafing through one of those perfect-bound pieces of hotel advertorial reading, a guide to 'the 100 best hotels of the world'.

'This isn't one of them,' complains Chris. 'It's a dump.'

'We should get Jill to keep this,' says Neil, meaning the hotel guide. 'Jill' is Jill Wall, their manager, who runs their office in London.

Chris looks around. 'All the hotels in America are designed for group sex. Glass surfaces. The hot tub. Mirrors. It's kink city.'

Sandwiches arrive. We are in Neil's room.

'I haven't got any sandwiches in my room,' Chris complains.

'It's the way he says that,' Neil says to me, 'as if he's got the worst room in the hotel.'

'I had a bath,' mutters Chris, 'and the cold tap fell off.'

They survey their schedule.

'I see Finland has been sneaked in here,' says Neil.

'I'm not doing it,' says Chris immediately.

Neil considers the cheek of it: 'One of these French interviewers is from Finland.'

'Slippery, aren't they?' grunts Chris.

The next interviewer is from *Express* magazine.

Neil's spiel again: '... the point of what we do isn't as performers. We are songwriters. We have put together a show which visualizes our songs...'

The interviewer muses on their unpopularity in France, the only European country where they have never had regular hits.

'I can't explain it,' sighs Neil. 'It's always very difficult to explain why you are or aren't popular. I think maybe we're too English.'

The Beatles were English, says the interviewer.

'I don't know,' says Neil. 'We'd like to be popular in France. We like Paris.'

'We're back into French fashion,' says Chris. 'We were into Italy for a while, but we're back. Chevignon, Chipie...'

There are now Chevignon cigarettes, the interviewer points out.

'That's so French,' says Neil. 'No one knows in France that smoking is bad for you.'

Neil shows me a few pieces of fan mail he brought from Japan. Maho says, 'It was very exciting concert! It looks like movie, because many scene make up one story. I'll never forget the wonderful concert as long as I live.' Miyako says, 'My dream is to live in London where you live.' Mariko says, 'Your dances are very cute! I never dreamed you danced such pretty!!' Yuki and Ryoko say, 'You're leaving Japan, aren't you? Your show have occupied a part of our mind for good. The meanings, the implications, the theme are too complicated to understand completely yet. But we never cease thinking about them. Yesterday we saw you at the disco "Gold". Sometimes we wondered if we should (or could) say greetings to you, however, we didn't dare to. If we bothered you by hanging around you in such private time, we feel so sorry ... Ultimate gratitude and thousands of kisses for you from Yuki and Ryoko for having given us so many dreams.'

More interviews. They field questions about 'How Can You Expect to be Taken Seriously?', a song deflating the pomposities of pop stars. They say there are five or six real-life models for the song. The interviewer pushes. Sting?

'Sting ...?' mutters Neil, even-handedly.

'He's a possible contender, isn't he?' laughs Chris.

'I don't think pop stars should get involved in important things,' says Neil. 'I don't think it's their role. I think they should criticize ... There's definitely a side of us that does things to annoy people, as a critique of the whole rock business. We always criticize. We're terribly critical people. We wish we weren't, really, because it makes life quite difficult. You notice what's going on around you and it doesn't necessarily make for a comfortable life. If people have comfortable lives they're almost not aware of what's going on. I think that's what makes for the comfort. We have a sort of funny pessimism, always expecting the worst.'

He sighs, then relaunches into further explanation. 'After a while the bullshit, the people not telling you the truth, starts to wear you down. It can make you angry, the stroking of ego. In America you have to do a lot of meet'n'greets – it's a deal you do so they'll play your record. They don't play your record because they like it, they do it because they've been paid, or because you've done them a favour. I think people in America feel it, but no one revolts against it any more. I think American capitalism is based upon a certain amount of corruption being acceptable, which I don't think it would be in Europe.'

The interviewer asks why they worked with Liza Minnelli.

'She liked "Rent",' explains Chris. He turns to Neil. 'Is that the official reason?'

'It's bullshit,' says Neil, and tells the real story, all dull record company machinations, then talks about the record. 'I was trying to make some of the lyrics sound like they might have been written by Jacques Brel, except in English.'

Chris starts talking about his new house, and about architects he likes. 'I like the attitude the French have. You can do whatever you want. In England you couldn't do that because Prince Charles wouldn't let you.'

You don't like Prince Charles? the interviewer wonders.

'No,' says Chris, 'I think he should be garrotted.'

Neil talks about some of his enthusiasms: Shostakovich, signed first editions by Graham Greene, late-Victorian paintings. The interviewer wonders if Chris likes such paintings too.

'Not really,' he says. 'I've got some modern art, but I just find art becomes decoration. I'm trying to design this house so it would work best without any art, without any belongings.'

Neil is asked about politics and soon winds round to his motor car theory: 'To me the main thing that is wrong in the world is people driving cars. We had a war because we were driving cars.'

'Neil can't drive,' Chris chips in.

'I think it's the fundamental evil,' explains Neil.

'You're the only person who thinks that,' says Chris.

'Yes,' Neil agrees, 'but I think I'm right.'

The interviewer asks about SIDA. AIDS.

'I think a lot of our songs have been about that. It's changed pop music completely, because pop music is about sex and AIDS has changed sex. Nightclubbing has become more about dancing and getting out of your head than a courtship ritual, and so dance music has become more pure. Disco was *sexual* – "love to love you baby", heavy breathing. Dance music now is heavy beats and you dance by yourself. These two things – that and the death of communism – have changed society entirely, and I think that it's difficult to know what to do or think in the aftermath.'

For his final question the interviewer asks about charity.

'We do a lot for charity,' says Chris, 'but we don't like to talk about it.'

Like what? he asks.

'I can't tell you,' says Chris.

The next interviewer is from *Salut*. He wants to know whether they're bored with granting interviews.

'You start giving the wrong answers because you're bored with the right ones,' says Chris.

'Or you say horrible things,' adds Neil.

They tell him this is their farewell tour.

You're splitting up? he asks, wide-eyed.

'No, we're not splitting up,' says Chris. 'It's the Farewell to the Fans tour.'

And welcome to what? he asks.

'Solitude,' says Chris.

They explain the tour's poor financial standing. They are budgeted, right now, to lose around half-a-million pounds. 'Now we can afford to lose a lot of money,' says Neil. 'It's an amusing way to go bankrupt.'

'The wigs are a thousand pounds each,' says Chris, 'and there's thirty-four wigs.'

'And,' adds Neil, 'there's a man to look after the wigs.'

The interviewer asks if Chris has been living up to his reputation by complaining a lot.

'I'm bored with complaining,' he says. 'I'm past complaining. I've become' – he grins – 'a much nicer person recently.'

The door bangs.

'It's only the wind,' says Chris and everyone chortles. The interviewer says that in France *Behaviour* was promoted with pictures of a Queen lookalike, its slogan 'The Queen's Favourite Group'.

Neil nods. 'They thought it was fabulously arresting, so we thought it must appeal to a French sense of humour.' In Japan, he says, they asked whether Neil and Chris would add to *Behaviour* a bonus disc of them reading their favourite fairy tale, supposedly to help the Japanese fans learn English.

Pete arrives with a new T-shirt for Chris. Pete is a friend of Chris who used to work for them and who is travelling on the tour. On the front of the T-shirt it says AMERICA. Chris has also just bought a new Mossimo hat, but he plans to hide it from the dancers until they leave Miami so that they can't copy him.

We head for a radio station, Power 96 – Neil, Chris, myself, the photographer Pennie Smith, Pete, their large security man and assistant, Dainton, and their American manager, Arma Andon. The Miami concert needs promoting – only 2,800 of a possible 5,000 tickets have been sold so far. In the limousine Neil plays some songs by their protégé Dave Cicero: 'Middle-class Life', 'Heaven', 'Then', 'Love is Everywhere'. 'All of them,' says Chris, 'are about failing with women.' He thinks a moment. 'We should market him as the new Bay City Rollers rolled into one.'

We pull up at the radio station. For a joke Arma gets out his American Express card and a bundle of cash and says, 'Why don't we just make this real easy? Two minutes. You can wait in the lobby.'

But they have to go in. 'Oh,' sighs Neil, 'the music business used to be a lot simpler.'

As we wait they discuss Trevor. Trevor is one of the two street dancers whom they asked to join the tour after they appeared in the 'How Can You Expect To Be Taken Seriously?' video. They think he has been shopping too much.

'We should pay him less,' says Chris.

'I think we do,' says Neil.

They are kept waiting for ages. Arma offers to do his 'nuclear management bit', but they decline. Instead they chat about Los Angeles.

'LA is our lady,' says Chris. 'It's about the only one.'

Finally the DJ introduces them: 'Neil and Chris from the Pet Shop Boys getting down with Cox on the radio.'

'Is that meant to be a *double entendre*?' asks Neil.

'What do you want to talk about?' the DJ asks.

'Tickets,' says Neil bluntly.

'Selling tickets,' confirms Chris. The DJ nods. 'We talked about our sexual preferences last time.'

The interview begins.

'So, Nick . . . ' he says.

'Neil, actually,' says Neil.

The next station is called Y-100 and there they are greeted by a man called Al Chio.

'Are both of you into Motown?' asks Al.

'Why are you asking?' says Chris defensively. 'It's a loaded question.'

'When I was growing up,' answers Neil, 'it was the Beatles and Motown. I used to like the Supremes.'

'Chicken supreme, I like,' says Chris.

As at most radio stations, they are asked to do loads of station IDs, whereby they introduce each of the station's DJs and various local campaigns. One of today's is 'Hi! This is Neil Tennant and Chris Lowe urging you to participate in recycling – everyone's help counts.'

'I did that one already for Japan,' says Neil.

'They should have recycled it, saved the tape,' says Chris.

On the way back Arma talks business, trying to get them interested in doing a Japanese TV ad and explaining what doors might open in America 'if "Streets" is a hit'. He pauses. 'And I believe it is a hit. But then I thought "So Hard" was a hit.'

They discuss the Katie Puckrik decision. Katie, one of eight classically trained dancers, was to have sung a song in the show, 'In the Night'. It was rehearsed, but at the very last moment, in Japan, they decided it didn't work and substituted a speedily rehearsed version of 'Rent', principally performed by Sylvia. *My Fair Lady* gets changed in Philadelphia,' they rationalize. 'That's show business.' Nevertheless, Katie didn't take it well.

Suddenly Chris announces, for no obvious reason, 'I like the morning. There's so much *hope* in the morning. There's so much potential, which is never realized by 8.30 in the evening.'

We dine at a Cuban restaurant, Victor's Café, with their American press agent, Susan Blond, Arma and Arma's wife, Alexandra.

'You get to do all the fun things,' Neil tells Alexandra in the car there. 'You get to go to the Seaquarium. We get asked, "What's a West End Girl?"'

Arma's children are here in Miami. They have been making friends with Dainton, though one of them said to Arma, 'I know why they call him Dainton – because he puts a dent in everything.'

'When did you discover you could sing?' Arma asks Neil.

'I only sang because Chris didn't sing,' he answers. 'Technically I'm not a very good singer.'

The evening is lost in old stories: Arma going to Spain to give Salvador Dali money for a sculpture John Lennon was giving to Ringo Starr; Susan Blond being filmed naked by Andy Warhol.

'Oh, Susan!' says Arma at this last revelation. 'That's something I didn't know about you. I'm so *proud* of you!'

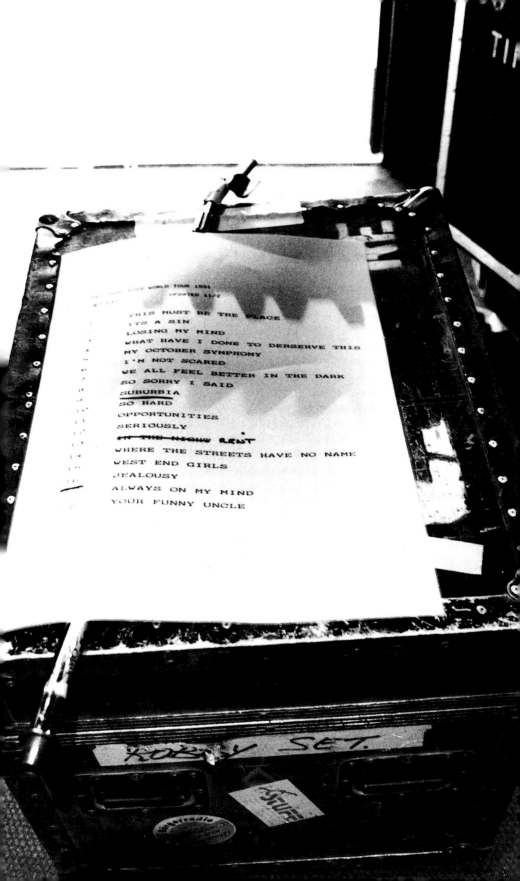

PET SHOP BOYS WORLD TOUR 1991
UPDATED LIST

THIS MUST BE THE PLACE
IT'S A SIN
LOSING MY MIND
WHAT HAVE I DONE TO DESERVE THIS
MY OCTOBER SYMPHONY
I'M NOT SCARED
WE ALL FEEL BETTER IN THE DARK
SO SORRY I SAID
~~SUBURBIA~~
SO HARD
OPPORTUNITIES
SERIOUSLY
~~IN THE NIGHT~~ RENT
WHERE THE STREETS HAVE NO NAME
WEST END GIRLS
JEALOUSY
ALWAYS ON MY MIND
YOUR FUNNY UNCLE

Tuesday, 19 March

Neil and Chris wander round Coconut Grove shopping for vitamins. Neil, who hasn't slept at all, is wearing a T-shirt saying MADE IN THE USA and bearing the Stars and Stripes. Arma takes them through some business. EMI America want to issue an edit of the David Morales dance mix of 'Where the Streets Have No Name' as their American single; Neil and Chris are adamant they shouldn't. Susan Blond tells them that Julio Iglesias's children are coming to the show tonight, and says that arrangements must be made for a party in New York.

'Doing the show is nothing,' sighs Neil, 'to doing the party. The show is a piece of cake.'

The head of EMI, Sal Licata, is coming to the show.

'He's bringing down his own photographer,' Arma explains. 'Record company presidents do not travel without their own trade photographer.'

'Why?' asks Neil.

'I guess he wants to take a photo of you and him,' shrugs Arma.

Susan explains that she can't get *Rolling Stone* to write anything about the tour. 'The entire staff want to come, though,' she says.

'Well,' says Arma, 'tell them to bring their pens.'

We arrive at the Knight Center.

'I like this venue,' says Chris. 'I'm sorry, it's a happening venue.'

The rest of the cast wander around. The music will be provided by Neil and Chris with three singers (Sylvia Mason-James, Derek Green and Pamela Sheyne), who dress as characters in the performance, and a guitarist (J.J. Belle) and keyboard player (Scott Davidson), who will play in the wings until introduced at the end of the show. Scott also operates the bank of computers out of which the backing tracks are generated. The musicians are fairly calm – they have done this kind of thing before – but the dancers gallivant around the backstage area in excitement. Eight of them have a classical background (Noel Wallace, Leon Maurice-Jones, Craig Maguire, Petee Aloysius, Sarah Toner, Suki Miles, Katie Puckrik and Catherine Malone). The two who don't, Trevor Henry and Mark Martin, were treated a little sniffily by the others to begin with, but it seems fine now. Also milling about is David Alden, the opera director whom Neil and Chris asked to direct the performance and who will be popping up on occasional dates around the country.

Someone asks Neil and Chris about the show.

'Something for everyone,' says Chris. 'Firm but fair.'

'Quick but tasty,' chips in Neil.

And after the tour?

'We're going to have a long holiday,' says Neil.

'And then we're going to open up a chain of chip shops,' says Chris, 'called the Chip Shop Boys.'

Then Chris notices that the backdrop of clouds behind the stage is ruffled and looks terrible. 'Those clouds have to be done,' he fumes. 'I'm not going on if they're not done. Or else the show's cancelled, basically. And that's the start of the American tour.'

A college radio duo appear and begin an interview.

'Hello, this is Kelsey and Wiggly D,' says someone who is presumably called Kelsey, 'and we're here with the Pet Shop Boys.'

'Squidgy Chris and Naughty Neil,' says Chris. He tells the interviewers, 'This show is completely different from any other show – unless you've been to see *Cats*.' They ask whether the Pet Shop Boys choose who remixes their records. (They do.)

'No,' says Chris, 'it's the record company.'

'They write the songs as well,' says Neil.

'We're just puppets,' Chris explains.

The interviewers ask about sampling and Neil gives a very considered answer about how 'people are always horrified when there's a new form of music, like when the electric guitar was invented, or jazz'.

'Everything new is good,' adds Chris. 'Even if it's bad, it's good. Because it's new.'

They ask why the Pet Shop Boys use so many one-word titles.

'We couldn't think of any longer ones,' says Chris. 'It's hard enough to think of one word, let alone a sentence.'

They sit in a backstage room, surrounded by wigs and stage costumes, preparing to be interviewed by MTV. Neil tries to sit on Chris's left.

'I always sit that side,' objects Chris.

'You do?' says Neil, moving over. 'I've never thought about it.'

'Shall I wear my glasses?' Chris asks him.

'Yeah!' says Neil. 'You're Chris Lowe! That's what you do. That's what you're all about.'

The cameraman objects that he can't wear sunglasses.

'Oh well,' says Chris, 'we'll cancel the interview.'

The interview starts.

'Do you think the US will have difficulty with this show?' asks the VJ, John Norris.

'People always underestimate American audiences,' replies Neil, 'say they want something safe. I think the success we've had here has been for having something different.' This is a spiel the Pet Shop Boys have picked up – that the new all-purpose compliment in young, slightly trendy America is to be 'different'. *Twin Peaks* is 'different'. *The Simpsons* is 'different'. The time was when you had to be wild, rebellious and out of order, when you had to stick up two fingers to the mainstream or wave your freak flag high, or whatever. Now, it's to be 'different'. If all these things can be 'different', maybe the Pet Shop Boys can be 'different' too.

The interviewer says that they have clips of the Pet Shop Boys for the last six years announcing they were planning to tour, and that each time the plans had to be cancelled. What changed?

'This is the show we always cancelled,' Neil explains. 'We just decided we could afford to lose an incredible amount of money; that's what changed. It's treated like it's a play, or a musical, or a ballet, or whatever pretentious word you want to use.'

They are asked about playing music live.

'It's never been a problem for us to create music live,' insists Chris. 'We're not about that pub band type of thing; it's about technology.'

'There's no tapes, folks,' says Neil.

So what is the show's plot?

'Well,' says Chris, breaking into a smile, 'I don't think anyone fully understands it, including the director. It's some weird journey for the Pet Shop Boys...'

'It's not like it's a thriller and you find out whodunit at the end,' adds Neil. 'It's a scenario rather than a story. At one point we thought of putting spoken bits in, but we thought it would be too precious.' Pause. 'We're angels at the end.'

'It's not very realistic,' says Chris. 'It's a laugh. There's this funny kind of prologue at the beginning which I don't understand.'

'Looks good, though,' says Neil. 'Our idea was to present an entertainment rather than an intellectually challenging evening.'

Are there any sexual moments?

'Not in America,' says Chris. 'They've been cut out. You only get them in Germany and Holland . . . '

' . . . and not,' adds Neil, 'if our parents are there.'

He asks about other people's concerts.

'You don't go to many, do you?' Neil says to Chris.

'No,' says Chris, 'but I don't go to the pictures. I don't read books. I'm a moron.'

They talk about shocking people.

'For some reason,' said Neil, 'it is impossible for us to shock people. It's amazing what you can get away with.'

'You just put it out in a press release if you want people to think it's shocking. We can't be bothered, and so even though we have sex and nudity in almost everything we do, we're never shocking.'

The VJ asks Chris to confirm that covering the U2 song was his idea.

'No,' says Chris obstinately.

'Chris, yes,' says Neil.

'No,' says Chris, lying, 'it was EMI's idea.'

The VJ asks about the video.

'It's set in the desert next to this funny tree,' drawls Chris. 'No, it's on a rooftop in downtown LA, but the police stopped it . . . It's got some go-go girls in the background, to make it a bit sexist for America.'

Neil compares it with the brooding drama of the 'Jealousy' video: 'There's no possibility of it being shown on television, but it's nice to show your friends.'

There are some supplementary questions. 'MTV is putting together a rockumentary on the history of heavy metal and where it's going . . . '

' "Rockumentary", if you will,' mutters Neil.

'That'll be a long programme,' says Chris. 'Heavy metal is to real music what wrestling is to boxing. Wrestling is this camp theatrical thing. I don't really regard it as music.'

'It's really the bastard child of glam rock,' says Neil, and pontificates on the possible connections. 'Although,' he adds, 'I have secretly written two heavy metal songs.'

They're asked whether they think that handing out free condoms in school promotes sex.

'Sex has never really needed much promotion,' says Chris. 'You really should try it, kids.'

A French TV crew takes them outside.

'I was told,' the interviewer says, 'you were scared of the public.'

'No,' says Chris, 'we despise the public.'

'Don't say that!' says Neil.

The interviewer mentions something about the press being rude.

'I'm going to smack their bottoms,' promises Chris. 'We're above criticism. We laugh in the face of it.'

'Do you think,' they are asked, 'you have changed, just a little bit, the face of popular music in the 1980s?'

Chris answers. 'We invented house music ... techno music ... industrial music ... that whole garage thing ... that Funky Drummer thing ... not bad going.'

They return to the hall. There is a problem, something to do with the different voltages in Europe and America, and there is a loud buzz.

'Are we officially worried?' Neil asks Howard Hopkins, the stage manager. He doesn't answer. They adjourn to the catering row for a pre-show dinner. It's chicken. 'Tom once said on Pan Am, because he was bored, we don't want chicken,' says Neil – 'Tom' is Tom Watkins, their former manager – 'and the hostess said, "But you must know, we're known as the chicken airline!"'

Robbie Williams, the production manager, appears, looking very worried. 'I don't want to underestimate how serious it is. We may have to cancel the show. We should work out a contingency plan; whether we can play tomorrow ...'

'It's doomed,' sighs Neil. 'It was obviously a dumb idea.'

'Well,' says Arma, 'welcome to America.' He smiles. 'See how calm I am? It'll only lose us $100,000.'

A security guard catches Neil on the way downstairs. 'Can I get your autograph,' he asks, 'before ...?'

'... before the show gets cancelled,' says Neil.

It's obvious, nevertheless, that no one really believes that it'll happen.

'I couldn't bear it if the show was cancelled,' says Neil. 'I just couldn't bear it. It's out of the question.' He stares at the stage. As technicians fiddle, a buzz switches on and off. 'Let's not stand here,' he says. 'I feel if we go away, a miracle may occur. There'll be divine intervention.'

We wander outside into the early evening sun.

'My intuitive sense,' says Arma, 'is that they'll have this solved in forty-five minutes.'

'It really is a crap start to the tour,' says Neil. He thinks. 'These things are always a cable,' he says. 'Not that I would know.' He sighs. 'This is so classic of us. We eventually get here, MTV is here, and we cancel the show.'

In the distance we can see fans arriving. Neil pretends to shout at them: 'It was all a kind of sophisticated joke! Obviously we're not *really* touring! We just go to a different venue every night and cancel the show! It's very situati –' He turns to me. 'What are those people called?'

The security guard stands and watches while Neil takes Polaroids. 'It could be an installation: *Miami at Night.*'

The guard says what a big fan he is. 'I haven't got your last one,' he apologizes.

'Well,' says Neil, 'that's your shopping list sorted out for tomorrow.'

'Shall we book a restaurant?' sighs Chris.

'I just ate some chicken,' Neil replies. 'That's the really annoying thing.'

'I just think it's dead funny,' says Chris. 'The show everyone's waited five years for, and it's cancelled.'

'Have faith,' says Pete.

'You gotta have faith,' sniggers Neil.

Jacob Marley, the choreographer, wanders past. 'There's a problem?' he says, clearly not appreciating the gravity of the situation. 'Oh *dear*. We can stay in Miami for another day . . . '

'Oh great, we can all go to the beach for another day, say the dancers,' mimics Neil, 'hastily unpacking their swimming trunks.'

'Maybe we were never meant to tour America,' Chris says. He laughs. 'Arma's good about these things: "Oh, the show's been cancelled. That's rock'n'roll." '

Lynne Easton, their make-up artist, appears. She is worried about the time. She doesn't know about the problems. 'Do you want to go and get ready?' she urges. Everyone laughs.

'I think they'll suddenly sort this out, because I'm incredibly optimistic,' says Neil.

'Well, you're the only one,' says Chris.

'They're eliminating some of the noise,' reports Arma, 'and then working on it for fifteen minutes and then you can listen to it.'

'I still think,' says Brad, their American booking agent, 'we should find the Dolby Noise Reduction button and press it.'

We go inside. Jon Lemon, the sound engineer, plays a Steely Dan record through the PA.

'I prefer the buzz,' says Chris.

Robbie runs past us.

'Everyone's getting a lot fitter anyway,' says Chris. 'We should get an expert in. We need Red Adair. The Red Adair of rock.'

It is now 7.45. They are due on-stage at 8.00.

'I haven't lost hope,' says Arma.

'No, I haven't lost hope yet,' agrees Neil. 'I'm mindlessly optimistic as well.' Chris laughs at him.

Jill Wall arrives. She has flown over just for this one show. As chance would have it, she's been talking to some fans who drove thirty hours from Canada to be here tonight.

'We should put them in a hotel,' says Neil.

'We wouldn't know where to find them now,' says Jill.

'Anyway, that's the least of our worries,' says Chris, 'our Canadian fans.'

The MTV producer comes by. 'We're getting lots of shots of the police in case there's a riot,' he says. No one laughs. 'Just joking,' he says.

'It'd be great television,' says Chris.

'And the next night,' Neil nods, 'we'd fight back, totally triumphant.'

Silence.

'Oh dear,' sighs Chris. 'Well, someone's really boobed. There's nothing to do. It's boring apart from anything else.'

They have a final listen to the problem buzz. It's still there, sometimes loud, sometimes not so loud.

'My view,' says Robbie, 'is that this is unacceptable for a quality show.'

'My vote,' echoes Ivan, 'is to postpone.'

'I don't think we want to start the tour with a disaster,' says Neil.

The decision is made. No show. Police are moved into position around the hall – all the fans are waiting outside and in the foyer. Jill is very unhappy. 'It's going to sound pathetic: they're not playing because of a technical hitch.'

'It is pathetic,' says Neil, 'but that's the way it is.'

'I think you and Chris should leave immediately,' advises Ivan.

We pile into the bus. Neil tries to hide before we pass the audience.

'We're going to get stoned,' says Chris.

They don't, of course.

'Well,' says Neil, gathering himself, 'it's very disappointing, I must say. It somehow seems incredibly typical that it should happen to us.'

'There's no use crying over spilt milk,' says Chris, deliberately deadpan, to much laughter.

'The ridiculous thing,' says Neil, 'is that it's nothing to do with the complexity of the production.'

'We've been shamed,' says Chris. 'We're publicly humiliated. The first chapter heading in the book should be America 1 Pet Shop Boys 0.'

Back at the hotel Jill says, 'Definitely stay in the hotel tonight.' It would not look good to be found nightclubbing after you've cancelled your concert. We go to the bar.

'How ya doing?' asks the barman.

'Oh,' says Neil. 'Actually, we're not at all.'

'Did I ask the wrong question?' says the barman.

'Well,' says Neil, 'it's the most disastrous day of our lives.'

The barman asks what he'd like.

'It somehow seems inappropriate to drink champagne. I feel it would be wrong to be discovered drinking champagne, so I think I'll have white wine.'

Chris appears from his room. 'Are we drinking champagne?' he asks.

'No,' says Neil, 'we're drinking white wine. We thought champagne was inappropriate.'

'Champagne, then, please,' Chris tells the barman.

We sit down. Pete knocks his glass and it sends about three more tumbling.

'Everything is jinxed,' says Neil. 'We should never have done this tour, Jill. Everything we touch turns to dust. The best thing we can all do is go to bed with a sleeping-pill. I think my star signs aren't in alignment.' He cocks an ear to the restaurant muzak. 'Mantovani,' he says. 'We used to have this record at home.'

Arma appears. They will play here tomorrow night. The New Orleans show has been moved back until Friday night.

The evening goes on and the conversation gets stranger. I overhear Neil talking to Jill.

'It's weird being us, isn't it?' he says.

'It must take a bit of getting used to,' she says.

'It takes more getting used to as it goes on.'

The talk opens up to the whole table and they chat for ages about U2 and pop success.

'You're as good as your last show,' sniggers Chris.

'And,' butts in Neil, 'we just cancelled it.'

Wednesday, 20 March

The problem is sorted out overnight.

'I've spoken to the people of Miami on the radio,' says Neil, 'and they understand.' He says he introduced himself by saying, 'I'm here to grovel before the concert-going public of Miami.' It is probably a smart move. Katie hears two girls talking in a Coconut Grove boutique about the cancellation, one saying to the other, 'I heard they were too wasted to go on.' When Chris hears these rumours he is utterly thrilled. 'Ace,' he says. 'That's *brilliant . . .*'

Neil is wearing an Armani suit; Chris is in shorts and a T-shirt.

'They're perfectly dressed as the Pet Shop Boys today,' comments David Alden, the show's director. 'It's the perfect look.'

At the venue Chris sends Pete to get me; Pete directs me towards a row in the production office between the promoter, Arma, Robbie and Ivan. Ivan is the tour manager. He is shouting, 'I'm talking about income and expenditure . . . This whole tour is running on my fuckin' credit card.' They are debating the financial repercussions of yesterday's cancellation. Ivan needs five thousand dollars in cash from the promoter, as originally agreed, for the tour cash flow. Eventually everyone but Ivan and Arma leaves.

'I love it. I love it,' Ivan sighs. 'If it's easy, it gets boring.'

Someone timidly knocks on the door.

'Yeah, come in,' he says. 'I only shut the door for drama.'

'Dead presidents,' says Arma.

'What?' says Ivan.

'Cash,' explains Arma. 'We call them dead presidents.'

Meanwhile Chris has decided he needs his own dressing-room. 'Suppose Neil wants to go to sleep,' he says, 'and also Neil's got into the habit of listening to classical music.'

Sal Licata's photographer finally wants to photograph them. Neil and Chris aren't keen.

'They'll try to do something sneaky,' predicts Neil, 'like issue it on the next twelve-inch mix.'

'He's got the best connections,' insists Arma.

'OK,' Neil concedes, 'as long as we see them and have copyright.'

Neil makes some derogatory comments about EMI, which I write down. Arma is horrified.

'What are you doing? We have a two- or three-record deal.'

'It'll be good when you want to get us off the label,' says Neil. 'You say, "Sal, have you seen page forty-three?"'

Arma doesn't press the point, instead saying, 'This was the easiest delay of a show I've known.'

'We're good at cancellations,' says Chris.

'We just cancelled for old time's sake,' says Neil.

Pete brings in some of the tour merchandise.

'Where did the black and green come from?' asks David Alden.

'Mark Farrow thought of it,' says Chris. Mark Farrow is their designer. 'It's the colour of the tour. It's the colour of money.'

Arma announces, 'There's a photographer outside' – Chris nods but says nothing – 'and he wants to take stuff and we can place it.'

'Neil,' relays Chris, 'there's a dodgy photographer outside and he wants to take photos of us and flog them for lots of money.'

They get dressed into the school uniforms and shorts for 'This Must be the Place', the first song. Neil looks at Chris approvingly.

'You're the kind of person who always used to look good in school uniform. I always looked naff.'

'I think everyone should wear them,' says Chris.

'Because there's no social distinction between people?' asks Neil.

'No,' says Chris, 'because they're sexy.'

'One minute thirty . . .' says Ivan. The American tour is finally about to start.

'You know,' says Chris as they leave the dressing-room, 'I've got a feeling the American public might not like this show . . .'

It's a show devised by David Alden and the designer David Fielding. 'We have a style we have evolved over the years,' David Alden had told me when I had interviewed him for the tour programme, 'a sort of dark, surrealistic, nightmarish vision of the modern world which we've used in various operas and theatre pieces. Somehow the Pet Shop Boys' songs seemed to cry out for the same sort of visual treatment.' They put together a vague storyline, a journey in which

the Pet Shop Boys travel from school to madness to popstardom to death, all the time battling with strange forces within them and against them, before finding some kind of rest. As a subtext Alden and Fielding imagined 'there's almost a kind of bet, and the whole fate of the world is being decided by what happens to the Pet Shop Boys on the journey they're taking'. It meant lots of costumes, lots of acting and, until the very end, no recognition whatsoever of the normal relationship between a pop musician and the audience. Neil and Chris had wanted their previous tour, directed by Derek Jarman, to be theatrical, and had achieved part of that goal. This time they intended to push it as far as possible.

But how will Miami take this? The lights dim, some classical music strikes up, and there are a few uncertain cheers. During the prologue, in which Katie plays with a globe of the earth, Derek is stabbed and Noel, dressed in much finery, shows the audience a large old book inscribed with arcane symbols; you can hear the confusion. Which ones are Pet Shop Boys? Neil and Chris appear as 'This Must be the Place' begins, at the end of a chain of identically dressed schoolchildren holding hands. It is an effectively un-starlike entrance. The two of them detach themselves from the others, but it is only when Neil begins to sing that most of the audience realize that the Pet Shop Boys are now on-stage. The other 'schoolchildren' hold up chalk boards which spell out JESUS SAVES. For 'It's a Sin' they change into nightgowns and are tormented by strange creatures. In 'Losing My Mind' Sylvia appears wielding a whip. After a short instrumental interlude Neil and Chris appear in their bowler-hatted moustached Magritte uniforms, carrying surfboards, for 'What Have I Done to Deserve This?' The female dancers wear pumpkinheads. During 'My October Symphony' Neil and Chris don't perform in the conventional sense (Derek sings) but simply appear at the back of the stage with suitcases and a camera, then move forward while dramas are acted around them. To their right Craig cracks open a giant statue of Stalin's head. After being surrounded by masked dancers during 'I'm Not Scared', only Chris remains on-stage for 'We All Feel Better in the Dark', stripping to his underwear, putting on training shoes and then dancing with Trevor and Mark as various obsessive cameos, sexual and otherwise, are acted out by the dancers. Neil and Pam duet 'So Sorry I Said', he in a strait-jacket and she in a wheelchair. The first half closes with 'Suburbia', Chris in a tiny cage and Neil also caged and sat in an electric chair. As the music fades away Trevor and Mark, dressed as sharp-suited gangsters with wings, machine-gun the clock above the stage and it explodes, exposing its inner coils and cogs.

★

There is an interval midway during the show. They return to their dressing-room.

'It seems to be going down well,' says Neil.

'The lighting's crap,' complains Chris. There have been a lot of missed cues.

'Don't be totally negative, Chris,' says Neil.

David Alden pops in. 'I think America likes it,' he smiles, but agrees with Chris that 'it looks visually shoddy'. Other compromises on the staging have been made without their authorization. 'I can just see,' predicts Chris, 'that it's going to get worse and worse until it gets to the stage where I'm going to refuse to go on.'

But how might they handle this situation with diplomacy?

'We'll get Dainton to whisper to Ivan that we're furious,' Neil decides.

'I think you need to threaten him with violence,' grumps Chris.

'You don't need to do that,' says Neil.

'It's the only thing they understand,' insists Chris, 'otherwise they just think we're . . . ' He never finds the word.

Susan Blond enters. 'It's the greatest thing I've ever seen,' she says before realizing that their mood hardly invites such comments. 'Are you not happy?' They say nothing. 'It's amazing. I was trying to figure out which things are lasers.'

'There aren't any lasers,' mutters Chris sullenly.

Howard pops his head round the door. 'Happy with everything?' he asks.

Chris merely glowers.

When he has gone Chris continues: 'We've got to get the idea out of people's heads that the tour is going to be fun. It's going to be bloody hard work.' He's also furious with the way some of the dancers played to the audience, particularly Craig's exhortation after cracking open the giant head of Stalin. 'It was like we've kicked Iraqi ass,' says Chris with disgust. 'He can just watch out.'

Pete appears. 'Whose idea was it to have an interval?'

'George Michael's,' says Neil. 'We stole it.'

'It's a brilliant move,' says Pete. 'They're screaming for merchandise.' He catches the drift of the atmosphere. 'Are you enjoying it?'

'No,' answers Chris. 'It's crap.'

Arma turns up. 'It's fabulous,' he raves. 'A thousand times better.'

★

The second half begins with 'So Hard'. Neil and Chris wear leather and wigs, their hair teased upwards in a ludicrous gravity-defying fashion, and carry umbrellas marked with a question mark. They change again for 'Opportunities' and 'How Can You Expect To Be Taken Seriously?' and parade more daft wigs, this time in the style of the most ghastly ginky eighties MTV pop stars. During the latter song Neil asks Chris, 'Do you have a message for your fans?' and holds out the microphone to him. Most times Chris will morosely shake his head, but tonight he takes it and says, 'Sorry about last night.' Sylvia's rendition of 'Rent' follows, then 'Where the Streets Have No Name ...' is performed as a Las Vegas show-stopper. For 'West End Girls' Neil commentates from the side of the stage in an overcoat while in the centre Chris drinks, fights and get sick. During 'Jealousy' they are pinned to the ground by two giant monuments in the shape of Oscars, and collapse, dead, in each other's arms.

There is a moment of silence, when the audience don't realize that the show is over, then hearty applause and screaming. They return as angels, perform 'Always on My Mind', introduce the cast and close with 'Your Funny Uncle', the two of them lying down on beds as it finishes, Neil saying 'goodnight'.

Backstage they seem muted. People keep popping their heads round the door: 'Incredible show!' 'Brilliant!'

'With a show like that,' says Brad, the booking agent, 'people will come and see you for ever.'

'That's good,' says Chris, 'because we're not doing it again.' They change. 'I think,' he sighs, 'we're contracted to go to a hospitality room.'

In fact, first Arma wants to bring down Sal and his photographer. 'Sal has flipped,' he reports.

'Ask for a million pounds,' says Neil.

Sal arrives and passes out congratulations with a well-practised enthusiasm. The photographer begins taking photos.

'Let's do it in the bathroom,' suggests Chris. 'That's more us.'

They line up.

'Didn't they love the oral sex?' Chris asks him – there is a moment between several pairs of dancers in 'We All Feel Better in the Dark'. 'I can't wait to get to Salt Lake City.' Sal looks nonplussed and mutters something complimentary about Sylvia's singing.

'We'll go upstairs,' Arma diplomatically breaks in, 'shake a few hands.'

Before they go Neil talks to Ivan. 'We've got to line up a meeting,' he says, 'because we, the creative ones, are horrified that you, the rock'n'rollers, are skimping on the detail. I think people think these are whims, but they really, really matter.'

Ivan nods. 'I understand. It's the details that make the show.'

Pete has been up to the meet'n'greet and reports back. 'No drink up there,' he says.

'I'm not going if there's no drink,' says Chris.

Down here there is champagne – it is in their touring contract that the local promoter provides champagne in their dressing-room – but not champagne that meets their approval. 'It's really crap champagne,' says Neil. 'Do we not specify the make?'

'French champagne,' says Ivan.

Up at the meet'n'greet some fans quiz Chris.

'Was everything live?' one asks.

'Yes, everything,' he says.

Another asks him to sign one of the T-shirts with Neil's face on it. 'You've got the wrong one,' Chris tells him, then proceeds to write upon it 'Chris Lowe (not pictured!)'.

Neil's hotel room:

'Neil's got a nicer room than me,' complains Chris.

Neil's bedside reading is *The Life and Evil Time of Nicolae Ceauçescu*.

Chris relates how a fan told him 'you make Erasure look crap'.

'There's a good reason for that,' says Neil.

Jill brings in a bottle of Dom Pérignon.

'It's that all-important word: expensive,' says Neil, and finally they celebrate.

Thursday, 21 March

There is a certain amount of drama as we leave the Mayfair House Hotel, everyone laden with far too much Miami shopping. David Alden and Jill Wall say their goodbyes for the moment. Pennie Smith discovers that her cameras have been stolen. It turns out that the hotel security have them, but have forced their backs open, damaging them. It is all very mysterious. After messy and inconclusive recriminations we leave.

'I expected us to be waved off by the Coconut Grove Traders: "Thank you for coming; thank you for spending," ' says Neil. 'The recession continues now.'

New Orleans, the Seaport Cajun Café and Bar:

Arma gives a potted history of the town, dwelling a while on tales of old absinthe houses.

'It's illegal now. It makes you mad,' nods Neil.

Chris perks up. 'Can you get it?'

Soon Neil and Arma are discussing American history. At one point Neil interjects, 'But you were doing something sneaky like siding with the French.'

Chris talks about wanting to travel between towns on one of the crew trucks.

'Why don't you ride around the block, get it out of your system?' suggests Arma.

'Chris was going to go youth-hostelling on his last holidays, with a back-pack,' Neil points out.

'A millionaire pop star backpacking,' tuts Pete. 'Ex-millionaire, after this tour.'

They discuss the tour deficit.

'I'll do anything to not make this tour lose money,' says Chris.

This time Arma's ears perk up. 'We'll find a sponsor,' he enthuses.

'I've done a big interview saying how we'll never do corporate sponsorship,' says Chris.

'You *didn't?*' says Arma, quite horrified.

'Yes.'

'When?' asks Arma, looking for ways to salvage the situation. 'Two years ago?'

'Yesterday.'

'You didn't mention any names, did you?' He's still trying.

'I talked about Pepsi and Coke.'

Arma looks a little downcast.

'Actually,' Neil says to him, 'we'd never do that.'

'It could be ironic,' suggests Chris, now he's out of the firing line.

'Oh yes,' says Neil. 'Ironic.'

There is a long pause, then Arma turns to Chris once more.

'Did you *really* do a number on sponsorship?'

'Yup.'

'Arma,' explains Neil, 'it's one of our big spiels. When "West End Girls" was out Sprite offered us a quarter of a million pounds. I rewrote the lyrics for them, and then we said no. Our manager was nearly in tears . . . '

'I hope you've learned the error of your ways,' says Arma.

'If anyone wants to make a donation to the arts – i.e. our show – and not get a mention, that's fine,' says Chris, trying to be conciliatory.

Arma persists, then Neil steps in. 'I think it ruins it. Look at Michael Jackson. When he did *Off the Wall* he was Pepsi-free and he was great. When he did *Bad*, which was also a T V commercial . . . '

'It might not be Pepsi,' argues Arma. 'It might be a product that was compatible in some obscure way.'

'I wouldn't mind that,' says Neil warily.

'Like, we're going to do a deal with Max Factor for Cathy Dennis.'

'It would have to be something very appropriate,' argues Chris.

'Like what?' wonders Neil. 'Condoms?'

'We don't have to get into who it is right now,' deflects Arma.

'I think we'd be better off sponsored by electrical products,' Neil offers, trying to be helpful.

'Maxell,' suggests Chris.

'Or Memorex,' says Neil.

' "Is it live or is it Memorex?" over everything we do!' whoops Chris.

We walk up to the Mississippi and see one of the paddle-cruisers go by. It is, we are told, the boat on which Culture Club filmed their 'Karma Chameleon' video.

★

44

Everyone is taken out to dinner at a place called Brennan's.

Neil watches REM singer Michael Stipe gyrate on MTV. 'I can't bear that dancing,' he says. He moves to walk back to the table. 'We didn't come here to watch MTV.'

The MTV announces that 'next up' is *MTV News*. Neil turns around. 'Oh, I think we should watch *MTV News*.'

At the end of *MTV News* is a fairly flattering lengthy sequence about the Pet Shop Boys tour which closes with some fans' comments: 'it's so cool, it's like a play'; 'it's a theatrical masterpiece'. Everyone is thrilled.

Friday, 22 March

'I don't really like New Orleans,' complains Chris, who has only been here for five minutes. 'It looks like another city in decline. I know it's the real thing, but it looks like a theme park, and every other shop's a crappy T-shirt shop. It's really sad. I can't really imagine anyone coming to see us in this place. When I look around I can't see any relation between us and here. I don't know why we're playing here.'

At the Saenger Theater Robbie calls a meeting. He says he's worried about the shows in San Francisco and Boston. The stages are too small, and he'd like the venues changed.

'It's not a very big market for us, Boston, is it?' says Chris.

Arma says he's not too keen to have them playing much bigger venues. 'The whole point of this tour is to have people outside who can't get in.'

'Exactly,' says Neil.

There are further, rather sharp discussions about the backdrop and the props and the missing snow and the costumes and the lighting. 'It worries me that we're negotiating the look of the show,' debates Neil calmly. 'It has to become a fixed thing. It's crazy. At the moment it's shoddy.'

'Basically,' sighs Robbie, 'we are doing a show that is too complicated for the circuit we are doing. And the theatre props are not designed to be thrown on and off trucks every night. We're going to have to keep spending. There's going to be running costs, to rebuild and restore. They spent the whole budget on one set of everything.'

'For sixty thousand pounds,' fumes Ivan, 'we get one dress rehearsal at the Brixton Academy.'

There is also a problem with the two musicians, Scott (playing keyboards and operating the computers) and J.J. (playing guitar). They are in the wings to the right as you face the stage; Scott can just be seen, but J.J. is completely hidden.

'I'm worried on a personal level – we did not employ them to stand backstage,' says Neil.

'I thought we did,' says Ivan.

'No,' Neil insists. 'We always meant to get them on the side of the stage or in the orchestra pit. I know J.J. is getting pissed off. It must be a bit frustrating.'

They run through everything. It turns out that the lighting problem is partly because the lighting is so complicated (790 cues, says Robbie; they have overloaded a console that is considered able to cope with anything) but largely because they are obliged to employ local spot operators at each venue. 'This country of yours, Arma,' sighs Neil. 'It's like Britain in the sixties.'

'Also,' says Robbie, 'it's designed with theatre in mind, where they have a three-day pre-light.'

'Yeah,' concedes Neil, 'but it's a theatre mentality we wanted for the lighting.'

Robbie suggests increasing the overall light level.

'You never can see anything,' demurs Chris, meaning at other artists' concerts.

'I never saw Madonna,' Neil agrees.

'It's just tough bananas,' says Chris.

'We should go over what you want in the dressing-room,' suggests Ivan. Neil has been complaining about the obligatory plates of cold meat: he can't bear the smell in such confined spaces.

'I think what it boils down to,' Neil explains, 'is some white wine, some water, and as many bottles of champagne as we can have.'

They visit a local radio station, B97. On the way Arma tells them that seven musical directors from radio stations are being flown in for tomorrow's show. 'Most of the schmoozing takes place after the show,' he explains. 'Kiss a few babies, shake a few hands and ask them point-blank if they're going to play "Where the Streets..."'

When they are led into the DJ booth the DJ is playing 'Joyride' by Roxette. 'OK, everyone,' he says, 'whistle along...'

'This is your first visit to the US?' he asks.

'Is it?' says Chris. 'No, actually I was born in Milwaukee.'

'You're *kidding* me!' exclaims the DJ.

'No, was I heck,' says Chris.

'Chris,' he persists, 'what's your summation of New Orleans?'

'Very pleasant,' he says. 'I like it. All a bit old for me, that French stuff, and it's a pity, all those tourist shops.'

The DJ invites phone calls from listeners to quiz Neil and Chris. The first is put on air.

'Can I have a pair of Sting tickets?'

'We've run out.'

'Oh. Can I talk to the Pet Shop Boys, then?'

Both of them shout, 'No!'

The next caller asks, 'Where did you get your name?'

'We met in a pet shop,' says Chris.

The next caller asks for Pet Shop Boys tickets.

'Would you like to ask them a question?' prompts the DJ.

'No,' answers the caller.

The next caller says, 'Can I ask you a question about my girlfriend?'

'Not right now,' says the DJ.

The next callers are two girls together, Cindy and Renee.

'I have three of your tapes taped,' says Cindy. 'You can ask my mom.'

'Which tapes do you have?' asks the DJ.

'I taped them off my friend's tapes,' says Cindy. 'I just want to tell them they're really, really good.'

'They say they appreciate it very much,' the DJ diplomatically interjects.

The next caller says, 'I want to compliment you on all your songs. They seem to comment on modern issues.'

'Are you coming to the show tonight?' asks Neil.

'I'm not sure I'll be able to get out . . . ' he says, then puts the phone down.

'Out of what?' wonders Chris. 'That was spooky.'

Then the DJ asks some banal questions of his own and they do the usual series of radio IDs ('Hello, Surf Club Live! We're the Pet Shop Boys!').

On the escalator back to the car Chris sighs and says, 'It's a bit depressing. One thing's for sure – I don't want to spend my life cracking America.' Later he adds, 'You know, I never want to go to a radio station ever again. I just can't bear it.'

But he will have to.

Back at the venue they discuss their forthcoming live appearance on America's most important chat show, *The Tonight Show.*

'I don't know if we shouldn't do what we normally do,' says Chris. 'Be a duo. Otherwise, on-stage you're going to see a Rastafarian guitarist and we're going to look like everyone else.'

'We've got Trevor and Mark,' points out Neil.

'Yeah,' says Chris, 'but that's not that different. For the Arsenio Hall show we had a scratch video made and banks of video screens and we had our attitude sorted out. We can't just plonk ourselves in front of a bunch of musicians. I don't want to be presented as us and a band. It's the wrong thing.' He thinks. 'We want lots of dry ice and smoke.'

Neil nods. 'It's got to look very . . . '

'. . . moody,' says Chris.

'Technical,' says Neil.

'Like we look like,' says Chris.

'We should be right next to each other,' adds Neil. 'We have to establish that we are a duo. We have to look like a duo.'

A man comes laden with bowls of salad. Neil and Chris tell him they don't want it and ask him to take it away, but he categorically refuses. 'I have to stick all this stuff in here,' he insists. 'You gotta tell someone big or else I'll get in trouble.' So they give in, he deposits the food and leaves.

'You can't not have food in your dressing-room,' huffs Neil. 'It's absolutely *de rigueur.*'

Downstairs there is a soundcheck. They go through 'Rent' over and over, Sylvia unhappy with Derek's harmonies, and Derek unhappy with Sylvia's criticisms.

'You always tell me different things,' he huffs.

'I'm not saying it's wrong,' she pacifies him, 'it's just not right.'

Chris is on the telephone in the production office, talking to the art director of *The Tonight Show* in Los Angeles.

'What we want out of it is something that looks like the Pet Shop Boys show – moody, lots of white light, maybe something extra like a flower strobe or a laser . . . *Everything.* As much as you've got, throw at us . . . I really don't know what your show looks like . . . If you're going for any image, kind of modern, industrial, technical. We usually perform in front of banks of video screens, but we haven't got anything to project on them now . . . It's a duo with a few extras, not a band . . . '

He re-joins Neil in the catering room. 'I had a word with the art director for *The Tonight Show.*'

'Who is he?' asks Neil.

'No one knows his name,' misquotes Chris. 'He said, "You have no creative

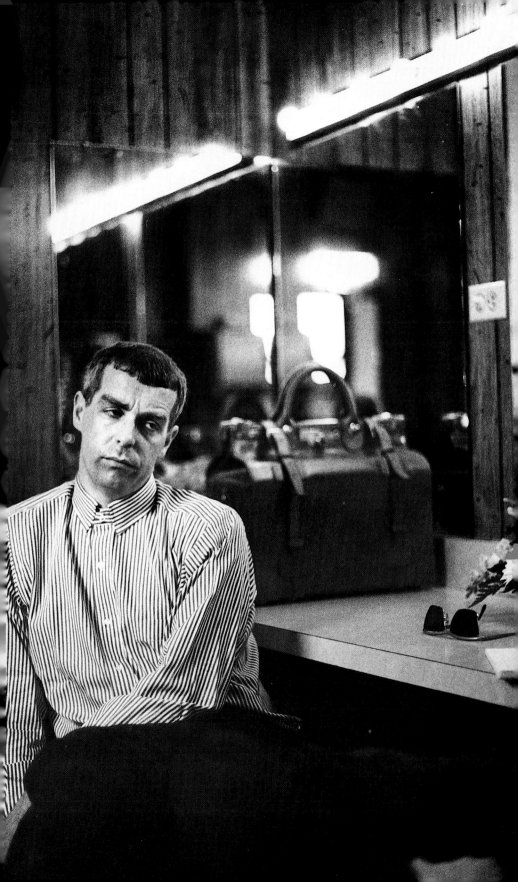

control whatsoever – get lost." ' He didn't. 'I told him we didn't want any close-ups of Scott playing the keyboards.'

'You told him that?' laughs Neil. 'You nasty.'

'I've seen shows when the main members of the band don't get shown,' says Chris. 'Duran Duran – Nick Rhodes didn't get shown at the Diamond Awards. Most people in America haven't seen us at all and they'll just think it's a band.'

They discuss clothes for the show. Chris is depressed that he can't find a good new wardrobe. 'I could wear my LA Raiders clothes,' he glumly reflects. 'I don't even know what sport LA Raiders is.'

Back in the dressing-room Neil picks up his schoolboy pair of socks and waves them about in a fury. 'They've done it again! Socks with different lengths.'

'We shouldn't swap socks,' Chris tuts maternally, 'because they can give you verrucas.'

'Five minutes,' says Jacob.

'Oh, it's such a chore doing this show,' says Chris. 'I think by the time we get to LA it will be treated like *The Rocky Horror Show*. I think there will be bits in the show where people bring out umbrellas.'

'Where's my pumpkin?' someone shouts in the corridor.

'Now you don't get *that* backstage at many rock shows,' says Chris. ' "Where's my pumpkin?" '

And off they go. Chris sighs in anticipation. 'I hate it when it's not fun,' he says.

Halftime:

'They're a filthy audience,' says Neil. There were wolf-whistles for the SM vixens in 'It's a Sin'.

'There's a horrible blonde woman near the front,' complains Chris, 'who's saying, "Come on, impress me." '

'Rather like us,' says Neil.

Chris wanders into the bathroom. 'Let's . . . take a pee,' he sings, to the tune of 'Suburbia'. He says he prefers the second half. 'The first half is really boring apart from "Suburbia".'

' "What Have I Done to Deserve This?" is good,' says Neil.

'There's that new bit,' objects Chris, 'your singers have added that we don't like.'

'Well, if you'd come to music rehearsals –' says Neil.

'I could have said it was crap,' interrupts Chris. 'Oh, it's uphill all the way now. Or downhill. Mind you, I hate "West End Girls" . . . '

'We think you should be actually sick,' says Neil.

'And then eat it off the floor like a dog,' says Chris. 'Like Divine.' He gets dressed for the second half. 'It's too hot to wear a wig,' he moans.

'It is *never* too hot to wear a wig,' chastises Neil.

Pete comes in. 'They're making people sit down when they stand up,' he complains.

'That's America,' says Chris, 'land of the free.'

When they come off-stage Dainton gruffly announces, 'Upstairs. Champagne already poured.'

'You're not supposed to do that,' scolds Chris. 'There's that all-important pop.'

Neil says he got the introductions wrong. 'They all said I said, "J.J. Belly". I'm the one with the belly, let's face it.'

Neil takes his make-up off. 'This is a new variant on a crap dressing-room,' he says. 'There's hot water and no cold water.'

'I'm going downstairs to check out hostility,' says Arma.

There is a rather surly German journalist down there.

'Did you like it?' Neil asks.

'To be honest,' he says, 'a few things I hated and a few things I loved.'

'Oh, just write about the things you loved,' says Neil.

The German then shares his insights with Chris. 'A few things were very good,' he imperiously announces, 'and a few things were very bad. I never saw the last tour, but I would have thought it was better . . . ' He complains about the pigs. He thinks they're like Pink Floyd. 'What I like about the Pet Shop Boys is a certain ambiguity, but if you talk about pigs there is no ambiguity.'

'I just think they look really good,' says Chris. 'I don't care what the symbolism is. And I like it when they start to eat us.'

Outside they sign autographs. One group say they're from Mobile and Neil says, 'That's in a Bob Dylan song', and attempts a brief nasal Bob Dylan impression. Chris has announced he doesn't want to drive to Houston as planned. He wants to go by plane.

'I can't believe that,' laughs Neil. 'Chris, who the bus was laid on for, is now going to fly.'

★

Public News, *Houston, 20 March, 'Pet Shop Boys arrive in the Land of the Big Mall':*
The Pet Shop Boys bring an extravagant stage show to Southern Star on Saturday . . .
I asked Chris Lowe if perhaps Pet Shop Boys songs like the elegant 'My October
Symphony' are the classical music of the future. 'I don't really have an answer for that
one,' he admitted.

Saturday, 23 March

Houston: Neil goes shopping. He buys a stetson and some cowboy boots. The local EMI promotions man is called Dan. He raves about a ballad on the new Roxette album, 'Spending My Time'. He says it will be number one for at least three weeks. He says he likes '... Streets ...' too: 'it's a different twist for you – so up and full of energy – and it's familiar, which is always in favour of the audience ...' Then he's raving about Queensryche's single 'Silent Lucidity': 'we're breaking new ground with that – it's six minutes and forty-six seconds; they're playing it kicking and screaming ...'

'It's not how long a record is,' mutters Neil, 'it's how long it seems.'

We head for KKBQ radio station. There are the parents of some fans in the lift. 'We've come to pick up free tickets. Our son will kill us when he hears.' Neil gives them a signed Pet Shop Boys postcard.

On the floor where the radio station is some fans appear.

'We've been waiting in the bathroom for about five hours!' they breathlessly exclaim.

'This is Jessica,' one introduces.

'Oh my God!' screams Jessica. 'This is cool!'

'So you've been potted up in the kazi?' confirms Dainton.

Neil does the interview; mostly the usual questions.

'This isn't a Texan accent we're hearing,' the DJ, who is called Jammer, notes accurately.

'No, it isn't ... y'all,' says Neil.

'Every time I meet someone from England I have to ask them,' the DJ continues, 'do you know Paul McCartney?'

'No, I don't,' says Neil.

It's over. Neil says to the programme director, 'Thanks for playing the records' and he answers, rather sweetly, 'Well, I haven't played them all.' Then when we leave he says, 'Hey, man, that's what it's all about – promotion in motion.'

We head straight for the Southern Star Amphitheater – a stage set in an open semicircular bowl. Close to the stage there are seats; further back is a wide grassy hill. Venues like this are called 'sheds' and hold around fifteen to twenty thousand people, whereas the theatres the Pet Shop Boys are playing average three to four thousand. Behind the stage is a funfair, which is included in the price of admission.

Neil looks around. 'There's no one here,' he says. 'I'm being a Chris Lowe pessimist.'

Chris arrives from the airport. 'Sheds!' he says. 'That's more like it. I think I've got the touring bug.' He heads off to try out the funfair rides. 'It's funny,' he says when he returns, 'I'm scared stiff flying, but on a fairground ride, which is much more dangerous ...' He moves on to an example: 'Someone got decapitated in Blackpool a couple of years ago. They stood up as a train was going towards a bridge.'

Neil retires to the dressing-room. 'I'm hiding from the *Der Spiegel* man.' They are annoyed with the German journalist, who is following them for one more day, because of his mealy-mouthed and arrogant concert appraisal last night.

He inspects the soft drinks on the table, clearly remembering the sponsorship conversation with Arma. 'This Must be the Sprite I Waited Years to Taste,' he says. 'It's a Sprite.' He reminisces once more about the amended 'West End Girls' rap he wrote five years previously. 'They'd done this ghastly thing so I rewrote it to make it more like us, more obscure. It was all about being on a beach, something like "on the beach and the surf / when the sun is up / you reach for the taste / of the freshest cup / the taste is Sprite ..."'

They have decided to give the German a formal interview, but only a short one. Ivan is told to tell him he can have ten minutes. He stomps in and rather sullenly says, 'I hear we can only do fifteen minutes.'

'Ten,' clarifies Neil.

The questions start out pompous and dull, but get better when he asks Neil about the significance of both Pet Shop Boys coming from the north of England.

'I think northerners who come to the south,' he says, 'have a kind of suspicion of the place, and also they have a different enthusiasm and attitude. Southerners, to generalize, are thought of as rather glib and they have everything. Northerners – rationing only ended the year I was born – aren't used to having everything ... But the north-east' – where he is from – 'and the north-west' – where Chris is from – 'have a completely different attitude.

People from Manchester, for instance, have a very strong, unique way of behaving – people talk slower and they're very self-conscious – whereas in the north-east people are more overtly fun-loving and open and innocent ... I think that when you come from the north you have a sense of wonder that you don't have if you're from the south, and I think that sense of wonder informs pop music ... '

The German asks whether Neil was glad he was old before he became successful.

'People have a limited career,' he answers, 'and it's sad when people are finished by twenty-seven, washed up, and they know nothing else. I feel I had a life before and maybe I'll have a life again. If we stopped being successful I wouldn't be very happy, but I wouldn't be washed up. I think it's made us much more level-headed.'

Doesn't, the German persists, a passion for pop music fade with age?

'It doesn't seem to,' Neil answers. Soon he is talking about his teenage theatrics: 'I was always fascinated by the theatre – I played in *Under Milk Wood*, I was in *The Merry Wives of Windsor* – I played Pistol – and I was in *Oliver!* I had the smallest speaking part. I think I'm slightly stagestruck, is the fact of the matter.'

The German asks about their planned musical.

'We're thinking about it,' says Neil. 'It'll probably never happen.'

Chris finally breaks his silence. 'We were going to do one called *Cheese*,' he relates deadpan, 'where all the characters play different cheeses. Like Camembert. It'd be a bit like *Starlight Express*.'

Why do people like them? asks the slightly baffled German.

'I think it's because they think we're different,' says Neil, 'and they like that we've got a sense of reserve about what we do.'

So what is the nature of their roles on stage?

'Well, the show is centred on us. We are the Pet Shop Boys. At the end we were going to say, "Tonight we were the Pet Shop Boys", but it sounded a bit pretentious.'

They tell him about Harvey Goldsmith's idea to run the show in the West End with other people taking their roles. The German wants to know who they think would be good.

'Vince Clarke and Andy Bell,' says Chris mischievously.

The German leaves.

'Strange, isn't he?' says Chris. 'I don't like him hanging around.' He looks at me. 'It's bad enough having one journalist.'

★

I talk to some fans in the front row.

'They're totally different from anyone else.'

'They're aloof, but I like it.'

'I'm going to move to London, because I hate America.'

'They have a cold tone, but it makes you feel good.'

'I like Neil Tennant's voice. He sounds kinda like Al Stewart.'

'They have black-and-white record covers and a sad look on their faces.'

'Their titles are so simple.'

'My aunt is a manager for Harry Connick Jnr.'

'They talk about love in a different way to most people. Everyone else is "love – it's the best thing, baby".'

'They have a lot of song titles that begin with "W".'

'I like the fact that they've kept the same image. You don't see that too much. Most people change who they are, like Madonna, but they obviously liked who they were in the first place.'

Backstage:

'Chris,' says Neil, 'there's twenty thousand Texans out there and we're going to come on in school uniforms and do some dirty dancing.'

'Oh well,' says Chris. 'It sounds good.'

Neil nods. 'We always tend to overlook that. That there is quite a lot of music.'

Some people have been telling Neil how they liked *It Couldn't Happen Here*, the Pet Shop Boys' film. 'So they probably will like the show: it's actually the show of the film. They go on a journey and meet lots of strange people. Let's face it: we've got one idea.'

They talk about album titles. Neil says that he suggested the Electronic album be called *Drug References*. They worry what they'll call their forthcoming greatest hits record. They consider *As It Were* and *The Importance of Being Pet Shop Boys*.

The orchestrated Pet Shop Boys medley of the overture begins.

'I've still got alcohol in me from last night,' says Chris.

'Did you go for it?' asks Neil.

'No, I didn't go for it,' he answers, 'but I got there anyway.'

'I think our songs work better as swing than electrodisco,' says Neil, listening to the medley. 'It's very Frank Sinatra.' He sings along, Sinatra-style. ' "East End boys and West End chicks" . . . Frank always sings "chicks".'

★

Halftime:

'It's a huge happener!' exclaims Neil. 'This is a show for the sheds.' The atmosphere is triumphant – from the stage there are people as far as you can see. Up on the grass knoll some fans have even started a bonfire, and in the outdoor Houston air it feels less like a concert presentation and more like a celebration.

'Superb!' says Ivan, bursting into the dressing-room. 'It's a rock show. It's a fuckin' rock show.'

'I like American audiences,' says Neil. 'I tell you what's good about them. They're not post-everything; they're still into things.'

Ivan tells them they're invited to an Oscars party.

'Maybe Sean Penn will be there,' says Chris.

'When Robert de Niro came to London,' digresses Lynne, 'and Bananarama had "Robert de Niro's Waiting" out they went to Zanzibar to meet him and he said, "Why did you call it that?" and they said because they couldn't think of anything to rhyme with "Al Pacino" and then they were sick on the pavement outside in front of him.'

'We should make a record with them,' says Neil.

Afterwards they are lined up with about fifteen radio DJs for a photograph. Instead of asking them to say 'cheese', the man from EMI who is holding the camera says, 'Everyone say "Streets With No Name".' Then he corrects this instruction to 'Everybody Add Streets With No Name'.

An incredibly long limousine ferries them back to the hotel. When they pull up there is a party of Houston socialites in incredibly swanky evening wear.

'There's nothing better than when there's loads of snoots outside a hotel,' says Neil, 'and a bunch of scruffs turn up in a limo. That's what rock'n'roll is all about.'

I am too tired to stay up, but they go off to a nightclub, the Lizard Lounge, to celebrate Ivan's birthday in decadent style. Chris does an interview with another radio station – 93Q – live from the club. 'It's kind of fitting,' he tells Neil in the morning, 'that you do interviews in the afternoon and I do one in the middle of the night.'

Houston Post, 25 March, 'Music takes second billing in Pet Shop Boys concert':
The Pet Shop Boys didn't put on much of a concert at Southern Star Amphitheater Saturday night. But the British duo sure put on one heck of a show . . . The Boys write

disco with a message . . . But the irony of the message seemed lost on much of the young crowd amongst the estimated 5,000 concertgoers . . . After two hours of such surreal pop opera, one couldn't help but pine for the good ol' days when a vocalist simply stood at a microphone and sang.

Sunday, 24 March

In the car to the airport Neil is feeling a little woozy. He says that a man from a radio station told him last night that their show scored nine out of ten. 'He only gave Sting three out of ten.'

We look at Houston, a little cluster of buildings against the flat skyline.

'It's like *Planet of the Apes*,' says Chris.

'It's like a mirage,' says Neil. 'It's a city totally built for cars. It's like a normal city, except on the scale of cars, not of people.'

'I like Texas,' says Chris. 'It's so big. How many times can you fit Great Britain into Texas?'

'I don't know,' answers Neil, 'but I'm sure you've tried.'

They discuss families. Chris's parents will be arriving in Los Angeles from England this afternoon. Neil's brother Philip and his girlfriend will be there too.

'For some reason I'm not looking forward to LA,' says Neil. 'It kind of depresses me, staying in the Mondrian again.' He sighs. 'We've only been away from home for two weeks.'

'I guess a year feels the same,' says Chris.

'No,' says Neil, 'a year would be like a lifetime. You have to hand it to touring – it completely divorces you from real life.'

Madonna's 'Rescue Me' comes on the radio.

'Count the clichés,' says Neil. '*I believe in the power of love. Rescue me.* You can just tick them off.'

'We must do our cliché record,' Chris reminds him. They've long joked of making a record stringing together every single banal pop cliché in one song.

Not everyone is flying to Los Angeles. The singers, musicians, Trevor and Mark and the necessary off-stage staff are coming – everyone else is going straight on to San Francisco. Those Los Angeles bound fly via Dallas. During our stopover Neil buys Richard Nixon's latest book, this week's *New Yorker* (he wants to read an article about Truman) and two *Spiderman* comics. He looks on the credits page and recognizes the name Chris Claremont from his days in the

seventies editing Marvel's British editions. 'I used to talk to him.' Then he has a shoeshine.

In the limo from Los Angeles airport:
'Off to be imprisoned in the hotel,' says Neil sulkily.
'You should learn to drive, Neil,' says Chris.

Neil decides they should hire the hotel conference room for a quick *Tonight Show* rehearsal – just some pacing around on a hotel carpet. He discusses booking a restaurant for tonight with Ivan. To get a good restaurant seat in Los Angeles it is necessary to use star power. 'If you get the concierge to do it he'll do a number about the Pet Shop Boys,' Neil advises Ivan, 'rather than you having to do it shamelessly.'

In my room I see another feature about the tour on *MTV News*. Kurt Loeder says, 'This show may not be rock'n'roll, but it sure is something', but ends with a snide comment about disappointing ticket sales. When Chris arrives at the rehearsal he is still smarting from it. 'It was a real downer,' he fumes.

They discuss clothes. They decide to get the men to wear black tracksuits, and Sylvia and Pam black dresses.

'Should J.J. and Scott wear hats?' wonders Neil.

'No,' says Chris, 'because I'm going to wear a hat, so no one should wear hats.'

Chris is tired and grumpy. He has just been trying to have a sleep and a waiter insisted on coming into his room to deliver a complimentary basket of fruit.

'They ignore the Do Not Disturb signs!' he shouts.

'They think they know you so well,' says Ivan playfully.

'It's not that,' explains Neil. 'They just think that fruit is so overwhelmingly important.'

EMF are playing tonight a few minutes away down Sunset Boulevard. Neil decides he'd like to go. The Whiskey-a-Go-Go, the venue, is still wearing the retro coat of paint it received as a location for *The Doors*, but inside there is genuine excitement, and EMF are just as ramshackle and petulant as you'd want the new rebel bad-boy pop group to be. Afterwards we go backstage. Jack Satter, vice-president for promotion at EMI's New York offices, who has flown in to watch the show, looks embarrassed and guilty. He hasn't bothered to see the Pet

Shop Boys yet. Ian Dench, EMF's songwriter, talks to Neil. The others look sweaty and exhausted, and don't say much at all.

Village View, Los Angeles, 29 March, 'Gotta Dance! The Pet Shop Boys' Chris Lowe Defends Dance Music and Ridicules Rock Critics':
The Pet Shop Boys aren't so much cynical as wary . . . It may be stylized jadedness but it's infinitely preferable to the trendy chants and slip-on love that are currently in vogue . . . Lowe, contrary to most of what is written about him, is not a quiet, retreating type at all. Funny, witty and a huge fan of dance music, he makes you rethink the equation that dumps such a large amount of credit for the Pet Shop Boys' success in Neil Tennant's lap. [Chris speaking] 'One of the things I've never understood is that when I was at university and we all used to go out to nightclubs on Friday and Saturday nights, we used to have a really good time dancing to the dance music, but we'd go back to our rooms and listen to Genesis and Pink Floyd. I used to wonder, "Why do we do this? Why can't we admit to liking the music we genuinely like?" We'd dance to it at night, then kind of pooh-pooh it the next day. It seemed very odd. I think a lot of people like music for the wrong reasons – for intellectual reasons or because of peer pressure or because they've read in a magazine that this group is really good, rather than admitted that they like Saturday Night Fever, which they genuinely did like and that most people did buy anyway. You should always be honest with yourself as to the kind of music you genuinely do like . . . *[discussing the undercurrent of sadness in seventies dance music, a facet he feels has escaped most contemporary revivalists]* There was a real pathos in the music which was what I liked about it. I've always liked kind of up music with sad lyrics 'cause it just gives this tension and melancholy to the whole thing. I think the message of the Pet Shop Boys is that it's not going to be all right. You know it's not going to be all right.'

Monday, 25 March

Chris appears in the Mondrian Hotel reception wearing a Michelin Man T-shirt. 'That's me,' he says a little sarcastically. 'I'm the Michelin Man. I bounce back off the critics.'

Neil appears.

'So did you go back to the Hyatt to wreck rooms with EMF?' he asks Neil.

'No.'

'Why not?' says Chris. 'That's the whole point of going to see EMF.'

'They're so cute,' says Neil.

'They're like cartoon characters, aren't they?' Chris agrees. He thinks a moment.

Neil sits down. 'The last time we were here,' he recalls, 'two boys jumped out of the top floor windows and committed suicide, flying past my window in the process.'

'There was a massive area of splattered blood,' adds Chris.

'They were still hosing it down in the morning,' continues Neil.

'Did you hear Living Colour on MTV?' Chris sneers. 'They were talking about how the message is just as important as the music.'

'So what is the message?' says Neil.

'They didn't say, of course,' answers Chris. 'My dad,' he begins, changing the subject, 'had twelve hours' sleep last night.'

'He *is* one of the Lowes,' Neil points out.

'They're going to Las Vegas tomorrow.'

'How will they get there?'

'They'll find it. I think parents are more capable than you think.'

Chris begins to worry about this afternoon's TV performance.

'We've got to tell Scott not to dance behind the keyboard.'

'Oh,' agrees Neil, 'they're not allowed to look, under any circumstances, as if they're enjoying themselves.'

'They mustn't move,' Chris summarizes.

'We've got to make sure we look like a duo,' says Neil, 'albeit with a few people scattered around. But you already told them that.'

'I'll be monitoring the monitors,' warns Chris.

We arrive at *The Tonight Show* and inspect the set.

'They've somehow managed to make high-tech keyboards look not high-tech,' complains Chris. 'It's because there's a carpet. Fancy having a carpet. I've never seen a carpet on a TV show. It looks like somebody's front room. It's so crap.'

'Well, let's face it, everybody,' says Neil, 'it's not as good as the Arsenio Hall show. No free teddy bears. You get a teddy bear with an Arsenio Hall sweater on.'

Yon, a man from Susan Blond's office, is here. 'Arsenio is quick exposure, the hit factor,' he explains. 'On this it's like you've made it, that sort of exposure. It's more of a testament to someone's . . .'

'. . . longevity,' Chris chips in. He is teasing, but there is nothing in his voice to let Yon know this.

'Yeah, longevity. He's been on for thirty-five years.'

'Do we have any reviews yet?' asks Neil

'You had a good one in Miami,' Yon answers, 'but it was in Spanish.'

Ivan says someone has to go back to the hotel to fetch Chris's passport.

'Why not Neil's?' asks Chris.

'Because you're performing as a musician,' says Ivan. 'Neil is performing as a singer, not as a musician.'

'Do we need to look at Trevor and Mark's dance?' Neil asks Chris.

'It's too late to change it,' says Chris. 'It'll be all right.'

They retire to their dressing-room, room 2105. Neil browses through *In the Arena*, Richard Nixon's latest memoir. Chris watches Pete play Tetrus on his Game Boy. 'I had to stop playing it,' he says. 'You dream about these shapes falling down, turning them round. You get totally obsessed by it.'

Marla – 'Hi! I'm from *The Tonight Show* office!' – enters. She needs their passports, to sort out the pay-cheques. She has a form that needs filling out. They are being paid as a speciality act. 'Like a circus,' says Neil. She wants to know who is designated as The Singer.

'I'm the singer,' says Neil.

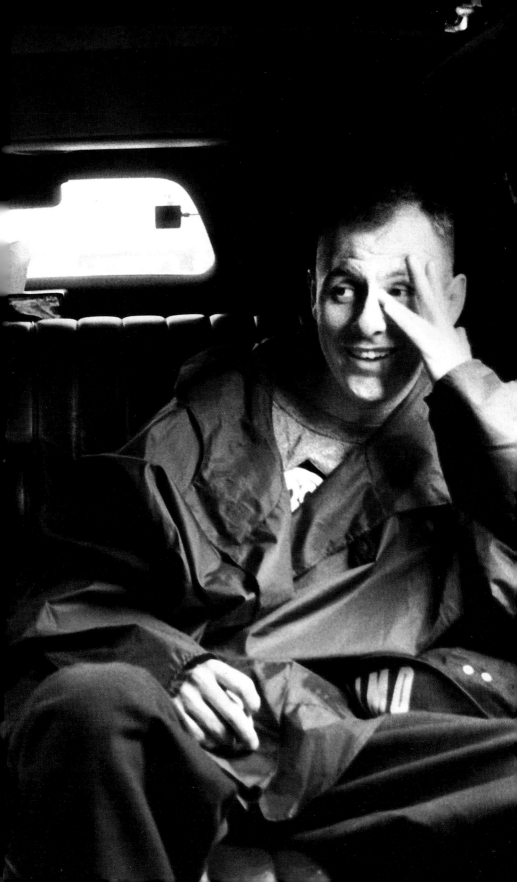

'Yes, you are,' says Marla.

'Ivan can fill that out,' says Neil.

'That makes me very happy,' Marla tells him.

When she goes they discuss American bureaucracy. Lawyers.

'Have you seen that advert on TV where you can contact a lawyer if you've got stress at work, and they'll sue your employer and get you time off?' huffs Chris. He thinks it's ridiculous. 'How many jobs *don't* have stress?'

Neil nods. 'That's what work *is*: stress.'

They quiz Ivan about details of today's payment. It's not as though the money is huge, but they seem to monitor all business dealings with the same principle: not 'how can we line our pockets?' but 'we don't want to be ripped off'. It turns out Chris will get something over $200, Neil something over $400.

'Well,' sighs Chris, 'I can't go on.'

Even the dancers, it turns out, get more than Chris.

'I'll dance,' he says.

'That'll throw a spanner in the works,' says Ivan. It's all eerily prophetic.

'God,' exclaims Chris, 'it's so boring. It's just so boring, I can't believe how boring it is.'

Waiting. Waiting. Chris yawns. 'I'm still not a hundred per cent yet. It normally takes me about a week to recover from a good night out.' He asks Ivan about tomorrow's flight to San Francisco.

'Delta,' says Ivan

'It's got the second-best safety record,' nods Chris, 'after Qantas.'

He asks about food. There is a canteen across the lot. 'Who pays for it?' he asks.

'You probably get a meal-ticket,' counsels Neil.

'The *singers* probably get a meal-ticket,' scowls Chris. 'Us musicians have to pay.'

Ivan returns. He has pointed out to Marla that both Neil and Chris were being interviewed, which has thrown her into a panic. Speciality acts don't do interviews. They are now being paid $512 each.

'That's good,' says Chris, 'upping our wages. Even though it doesn't matter. It's the principle of the thing.'

Back in the dressing-room the show's researcher, Debbie, comes to do the pre-interview. This is a common chat-show routine. The researcher finds out a few good stories for the on-screen interviewer to head towards. Tonight's host is not Johnny Carson but his occasional stand-in, Jay Leno, who is being groomed to take over full-time in a few months.

Is that overdone, Debbie asks, the journalist and the architect?

'Yes,' says Neil.

She moves on. 'I know this is overdone,' she says, 'but where did you meet?'

'I think people must know,' Chris mutters. 'I don't care if they don't.'

Neil tells her anyway.

'Have you done Marvel Comics to death?' she asks Neil. He used to edit British editions of Marvel Comics in the mid-seventies.

'No, not too much. That's kind of virgin territory.'

Neil suggests that Jay Leno should ask about their live show, and why they've never toured. 'We've been described as the most successful group that never tours.'

'OK,' says Debbie. 'That's good. How come?'

'That's what we'll tell you,' says Chris.

'We think that normal rock concerts are a bit boring,' says Neil.

'I don't know how many concerts he's been to,' says Debbie, meaning Jay Leno. 'Do you know who he is?'

'No,' says Chris.

'Do you know what he looks like?' she says.

'No,' says Chris.

'Be honest,' she says. 'Have you ever seen *The Tonight Show*?'

'Yes,' says Neil.

'From beginning to end?'

'No.'

The pre-interview continues. 'Jay will have a tendency ...' says Debbie, 'he will want to know where you're from. He asks everyone that, no matter where they're from. I have it written down.' She consults her notes. 'Where's Blackpool? I'm sure Jay's house in Britain is near there. Is it beautiful?'

'No,' says Chris.

'So did you like it?'

'Yeah, but I don't just like things that are beautiful. I like things that are ugly.'

Slowly, Chris loosens up a little. 'My grandmother's favourite show when she lived here,' he tells Debbie, 'was *The Tonight Show*, and it's the one thing she missed when she moved back ... My mother is in the audience tonight.'

'Oh,' says Debbie, 'that's good.'

'My mother was a dancer,' Chris tells her.

'Then she met your dad,' interjects Neil, 'and he said, no dancing.'

'Sort of,' Chris says. 'Now she's a housewife.'

'They're still together?' Debbie asks.

'Oh yes,' says Chris. 'We're English. We don't get divorced.'

Waiting for the rehearsal, I talk to Pennie Smith. She is fretting. The Pet Shop Boys keep flying between concerts. Hotel – limousine – airport – plane – airport – limousine – hotel. No photos.

'It's a pity they don't do drugs,' she sighs, 'because then they'd travel by bus everywhere.'

A director fusses round in an avuncular yellow jumper.

'I just want to make one thing clear,' Neil tells him, indicating towards Trevor and Mark. 'They're wearing black suits with wings on.'

'Their own or props?' the director asks.

Scott fiddles with the computers. There is a crisis, if something as insignificant as a click on the timbali sample could be called a crisis.

'Do you want smoke on both songs?' shouts the director.

'We always want smoke,' Neil responds. 'We're the Pet Shop Boys. That's what we're all about.'

Jay Leno bounds on to the set.

'Hi, guys! I'm Jay. How are you? Where are you both from? Get the bubble'n'squeak for these boys!'

No laughter.

'No one knows what I mean,' he mutters, though of course everyone knows precisely.

Chris's keyboard is moved more centrally. Neil and Chris are worried about emphasizing they are a duo.

'They're bound to stitch us up anyway,' predicts Neil. 'If a TV director doesn't want to show something, he doesn't.'

Back in the dressing-room we watch the NBC internal live TV feed outside the Oscars ceremony. It's funny, because you see all the cameramen touching up their hair, picking their noses and fighting to get interviews with the same stars.

'This is so much better than the proper coverage,' says Chris.

'It's very Andy Warhol,' agrees Neil. 'You just have a camera and there's all these stupid people standing around talking drivel. This is what they live for, the Oscars. They're all in a tizz.' There's an Oscar party at our hotel tonight. 'I'm thinking of complaining about the noise at about one o'clock,' Neil says, 'and then demanding a refund on my room. I might call the police.' Within two minutes he has rather changed his tune. 'I'm sorting out us producing Madonna's next album tonight. That's what I'm doing. Starting October 1st – write the songs in September, out in March.' He fakes a resigned sigh. 'Oh, she can *pretend* to write the blasted songs and have a third of the royalties.'

His eyes return to the TV. 'Why doesn't some serious movie star like Liz Taylor arrive?' He considers this. 'Actually, serious film stars don't make films, do they? They're sort of beyond that.'

'I'm not interested in the movie business,' Chris interrupts. 'There's much better things than going to the pictures.' He went to see *New Jack City*, but that was 'because there's riots at the cinema'.

Debbie returns.

'Do you want some oranges?'

'I hate oranges,' says Neil.

'Do you want anything?'

'No,' says Neil, 'we're fine. We're unusually content.'

She leaves.

'Actually, they're quite nice here,' says Neil. 'I hate to say it, but they're quite nice.'

Ivan comes in. 'OK. Here we go. It's contract time.'

Neil and Chris pore over the contracts.

'My gross income?' splutters Neil. 'It's none of their bloody business!'

Chris looks back up at the Oscars screen.

'The funny thing about these things is you always have to queue up. They're doing it here. It's like that Michael Jackson thing we went to.'

'It's always chaos,' says Ivan, 'because everyone's a celebrity.'

'It's not like you get there, get your Oscar and have a drink.'

Talk drifts on to actors.

'Who is it who listens to "West End Girls" to get into character?' Neil asks us to remind him, but no one knows.

'We don't like him,' Neil prompts. Still can't remember. 'Mickey Rourke!' he eventually exclaims. 'He did it for *Angel Heart*.'

On screen Jon Bon Jovi wanders by.

'Is he appearing in it?' asks Chris.

'He's doing "Blaze of bleedin' Glory",' harrumphs Neil. Dainton tells us about the time he met Jon Bon Jovi's mother. 'She knows Debbie Gibson's mother,' he tells us.

Neil goes to the toilet. When he comes back all the chairs are taken.

'Oi!' he addresses Ivan. 'Can I sit down?' Ivan quickly rises.

'Shame on you, Neil,' mutters Pete. 'Pulling rank.'

Debbie returns with a typed sheet of information and questions about the Pet Shop Boys.

'You guys, this is what I give Jay. You're going to have a tendency to laugh at it because it looks silly.'

In a way it does. There are six questions and, after them, the gist of what Jay can expect the Pet Shop Boys to say:

YOU GUYS HAVE HAD HUGE SUCCESS OVER THE PAST 5 YEARS – SOLD OVER 15 MILLION ALBUMS. BUT YOU HAVE NEVER TOURED. HOW COME?

Quite honestly they think most rock concerts are boring and they didn't want to be.

I UNDERSTAND YOUR SHOW IS VERY THEATRICAL . . . TELL ME ABOUT IT . . .

They've worked with opera and theater people to put together a special show. They have 10 dancers – 8 classical and 2 street – in the show. They brought the 2 street dancers here – which you can joke with them about.

YOU'VE PLAYED 3 DATES ALREADY IN THE US – HAS EVERYTHING GONE SMOOTHLY?

No. Their first date in Miami had to be cancelled because of bad sound system. They were depressed to be seen in public – but saw the humor in it the next day.

YOU GUYS LIVE IN ENGLAND. HAVE YOU SEEN THE TONIGHT SHOW BEFORE? AN *ENTIRE* SHOW?

They've seen The Tonight Show, *but will admit not a whole one.*

WHERE ARE YOU FROM ORIGINALLY?

Chris is from Blackpool, England, which he'll say is not a very pretty place. Neil is from Newcastle, a mining community.

CHRIS, SOMEONE TOLD ME YOU COME FROM A FAMILY OF SHOW BUSINESS. YOUR MOM? AND YOUR GRANDFATHER?

His mom, who is in the audience, used to be a dancer and his grandfather was one of the Nitwits – a comedy jazz band who appeared in Vegas for 6 years.

WILL YOU DO ANOTHER SONG FOR US . . .

The dressing-room screen switches to the downstairs studio. Filming has begun, with the famous *Tonight Show* host monologue: a chain of light, topical jokes. Jay Leno says Sinead O'Connor has got a part in a film as Joan of Arc 'but they're worried that they'll cheer when she's burnt at the stake'.

'That's moderately amusing,' says Neil.

Time to go. Jay Leno introduces them: 'They've sold over fifteen million albums! And it's only Monday . . .'

It is at first with astonishment, then with horror, that from the side of the stage the rest of the entourage watch the filmed performance of 'Where the Streets Have No Name' on the backstage monitor. The opening shot is framed so that you see Neil and, behind him, the three backing singers. Then . . . just the same. The shot doesn't change. A minute passes. The shot still doesn't change. To anyone watching all over America who doesn't know much about the Pet Shop Boys – most of them – the Pet Shop Boys are a singer and three backing vocalists. It gets worse. Trevor and Mark do their dance and Trevor slips over. Chris has had enough. It later turns out he has been watching the fiasco himself on a monitor he can see from the stage and knows the camera has barely set its eyes on him. He strides across the set and into the wings, mid-song. The others, unsure what to do, continue.

'I said this would happen,' he fumes, at the side of the stage. The song is still playing.

'Let's go,' says Pete.

'I might as well wait till the end,' says Chris.

Debbie is sympathetic. 'I can't apologize to you enough. That fuckin' director.' She tries to persuade him to stay for 'How Can You Expect To Be Taken Seriously?' and suggests they'll reshoot the first. 'My point is, it makes you not look good.'

'I don't want to do another song,' Chris says. Then, in the entourage's general direction, 'I'll see you back at the hotel.'

Debbie rushes off. 'Let me see if I can get it reshot.'

Helen Kushnick, Jay Leno's manager, is fuming. 'Acting the way he did is not the way to behave. Walking off-stage in the middle of a number is totally unprofessional. You just don't do it.' She suspects it was a planned stunt, done on purpose.

Chris, Pete and Dainton sit in the dressing-room.

'The security man was impressed,' Chris sniggers. 'He said, "Cool, man, cool."'

'Do you want to go down and do the second number?' Dainton asks.

'I'm not doing the second number until we do the first number again.' From the exchanges I hear backstage Chris's hunch – that if he records the second number they will still refuse to shoot the first – is quite correct. 'Do the second number!' he huffs. 'They must think I'm completely stupid.'

Silence. Down on-stage the song has finished and Neil has looked around for a cue. Both of them were supposed to join Shelley Winters and Jay Leno for a chat. When Jay beckons him over he doesn't know what else to do. He fields questions, and takes a glass of water from the table in front of him. It is Shelley Winters's. It is whisky.

In the dressing-room I break my silence. I feel it is impossible to stay impassive. I don't think Chris has done the wrong thing, but the implications are mushrooming and to say nothing here and now in this atmosphere isn't to stay out of it, it's to offer more unequivocal support than my conscience can allow. I suggest to Chris that maybe Neil is going to feel a bit stitched up.

'Neil can get lost,' says Chris. 'Everyone can get lost.'

Later Pete will lecture me about this intervention, tell me my job is to watch, not intervene, tell me I was totally out of order.

'Actually, they're not going to re-record this,' Chris realizes. 'Let's just go.'

'Let's go,' echoes Pete.

Debbie returns, tries to cajole Chris to stay.

'It doesn't even make any difference if I'm there or not,' fumes Chris.

She is sympathetic about the whole matter. 'I agree with you one hundred per cent. I don't blame you for being upset.'

'I'm not upset,' Chris snaps. 'I just won't tolerate being treated like that.'

'You were right,' she says. 'I'm sorry. I'm really sorry. We're going to get shit.'

'*We're* not,' says Chris.

It is the commercial break – though the show is being taped for transmission later this evening, it is, like most American chat shows, recorded in real time, including commercial breaks – and Neil appears. The mood is tense. There is little time to sort anything out.

'I can't do the second number without you,' he tells Chris.

'You can,' says Chris. 'I wouldn't be seen anyway.'

'That wasn't my fault,' Neil says.

'I'm not saying it's your fault,' says Chris.

Chris and Pete leave. Neil returns to the stage. After the show, embarrassed, he apologizes to Leno. 'I'm sorry. What can you do? He has an incredibly hot temper.'

Back in the dressing-room Neil looks upset.

'So what do we think about all this?'

'The problem is,' says Ivan, 'that that woman with a hat' – Jay Leno's manager – 'lost her temper. She thinks the whole thing was set up, that we had given Chris a cue and he has walked off...'

'They were going to reshoot it anyway, is the joke, because the dancers fell over,' says Neil.

'They said, "No one walks off *The Tonight Show*",' Ivan tells him, ' "and gets reshot. We've been going for twenty-one years and that's never happened." '

'Of course Chris totally lost his temper too,' says Neil.

'He wasn't screaming,' Ivan points out. 'She was. She was saying, "Whose fuckin' record company is this? Someone's going to swing for it." '

Debbie returns. 'I just wanted to say how sorry I was...'

'We want to clarify,' Ivan tells her, 'that this was not a set-up...'

'I said to the director,' she says, ' "Did you know that Neil and Chris were the Pet Shop Boys?" and he says he was just about to give a cue. Chris should have maybe said, "Could we reshoot?" '

'But Chris is so suspicious that he thinks –' says Ivan.

'They would have reshot it,' she interrupts, 'if he had not walked off. But we have egos involved here.'

'I couldn't decide whether to stop singing or not,' says Neil.

'You did the right thing,' Debbie assures him, 'to be professional. But we're dealing with egos and institutions and inflexibility and I don't blame him.'

'As it happens,' says Neil, 'I do, because I blame him for dropping me in it...'

'He was right to be upset,' Debbie summarizes, 'but he didn't handle it well and we didn't handle him not handling it well ... Obviously you're artists and he's temperamental and he lost his cool. I don't know him, but I saw his chin shaking...'

Jay Leno's manager walks in. She spots me taking notes. 'Don't use my name or I'll sue you...'

Neil sighs.

'The really really really really really really really annoying thing is that Chris said, "They're going to shoot us like it's a band and not as if it's a duo", and we said, "Let's phone them up."'

'There's no doubt about it,' agrees Debbie, 'that they fucked up. Jay agreed, but Helen does have an ego . . .'

'Yes, and Chris having walked off, she thought Chris was blackmailing them. I appreciate she thinks, it's *The Tonight Show*, this is an American institution, who is this twerp? But on the other hand it's just a TV show. It's not the presidency.'

'His mother,' says Debbie, 'was appalled. She said she couldn't believe it from a show-business family.'

'If they hadn't been there he would have gone during the first verse,' says Neil. 'I wish I'd stopped singing, because as it is I muffed up the singing because I was thinking about it.'

'We must learn something from this,' Debbie announces. 'What can we learn?'

'The show must go on,' proclaims Ivan.

'That we should listen to people,' says Neil. 'Sometimes you have an instinct about it. I didn't, but Chris was worried about it from the start, because it's the first time we've appeared live with a band.' He sighs once more.

'Tell Chris I'm sorry,' says Debbie.

'He's going to be in a complete state,' says Neil.

'Call me tomorrow if you like,' suggests Debbie, 'and we can have a therapy session.'

Some fans run up to Neil as we leave.

'We think it's kinda fun,' they say. 'For us PSB fans we kind of get a kick out of it, because it's a thrill just to get you on our TV sets.' At the time, the way they say it, this is quite genuinely moving.

'It's nice of you to say that,' says Neil. 'It was kind of a great moment in rock at the end of the day. In twenty years' time when they make the film they'll be re-creating it.'

We drive back to the Mondrian. 'We haven't heard the last of that,' says Neil in the car.

'Arma's going to be screaming at me,' predicts Ivan.

'I don't care about *The Tonight Show* or being on a blacklist,' says Neil. 'I just care about being seen on TV by twenty-three million people sounding bad.'

'I suppose we should have known he was in a mood,' says Ivan, 'because Pete said this morning Chris wouldn't do it.'

Neil is surprised. 'He didn't discuss it with me. I was waiting in my room for The Trauma.'

'He was having second thoughts about doing it with the band,' says Ivan.

Neil sighs. 'It's Chapter 5. It's World War II. It's only been a week: we've cancelled a show and walked out on *The Tonight Show.* It's like the Sex Pistols' final tour.'

Back in the hotel everything feels very wrong, very bad. Neil asks me up to his room for a drink. He now feels very let down by the affair. 'Chris is so selfish,' he says. 'I sometimes wonder whether it's worth it.' It is the fourth time Chris has done something of this sort: he walked off the 'Rent' video in 1987, off the stage at the Tokyo Budokan in 1989 and at the end of *Wogan* in 1990. Neil gets maudlin, starts talking as though this is the end of the Pet Shop Boys. I am shocked. I've never seen him like this. For the second time today I decide that there is no neutral position: to say nothing is to encourage events in the direction they are heading. I tell him Chris hadn't meant to slight him, and nor had he flown off the handle; I tell him he had been forced into an impossible situation by the backstage ultimata.

Ironically, it is by finding some common ground of defiance that Neil begins to come round. Ivan phones to see how Neil is, and to get guidance as to how to deal with any repercussions. 'I don't want anyone offering snivelling apologies. I want to be totally up about it. I want Arma and Susan Blond – as our *employees* – to be totally up about it . . .' These are feelings he doesn't mind so much. This is a fight they know and like: Pet Shop Boys against the useless, snivelling, half-hearted, face-saving, insincere, unprincipled world.

And so, by the time he has finished talking to Ivan, he decides to call Chris. 'He'd just never call me,' he sighs. He knows there is no chance of even a fraction of an apology for what happened to him, the embarrassment he suffered in the slipstream of events. Chris's logic is rigorous. If he is wronged he will react in the most simple, straightforward way to address that. Those around him should realize that. If there are consequences to his actions they should blame those who wronged him, not him.

Chris bounces cheerfully into Neil's room. It's decided. They'll laugh about it, complain about the world together. Chris has just been with his parents. They haven't mentioned a thing.

'Your mother isn't talking about it?' chuckles Neil. 'That's so funny.' The last time she didn't talk about something like this was when the Pet Shop Boys were on *Saturday Night at the London Palladium* performing 'Rent' and they both refused to parade on at the end, as is tradition, and wave alongside Jimmy Tarbuck. She simply never mentioned it to Chris. If you don't talk about it, it doesn't exist.

The two of them discuss what they'd do if it happened again. Neil says Chris should have walked forwards, towards the cameras, so that they had to stop shooting.

'I'm not going to do that in front of all that audience,' says Chris.

And they talk about their plans for the evening. Neil is going to the Mondrian Oscars party: Chris is also invited but doesn't fancy it. They both joke again about phoning up, complaining about the noise.

'Don't get exceedingly drunk,' Chris counsels Neil.

'Chris, I'm likely, in the aftermath of this, to do something terrible. It'll be Naughty Neil. You know, every two or three years I start a fight ...' 'Naughty Neil' is what he was once called in the *Sun*, after an incident at the BBC bar in White City.

'That's what America needs,' Chris laughs. 'Naughty Neil.'

Neil, Dainton and I go to some Oscar parties. Our first stop is the Mondrian's own party, but, although Anjelica Huston is wandering around, it doesn't seem very star-studded. We meet this couple who suggest we try the Roxbury and handle everything at the door. We assume they are well connected. It is only later we discover that they aren't connected at all and that they get us all in everywhere on the strength of the name the Pet Shop Boys.

At the Roxbury we are seated by a window in the VIP section. Gregory Peck is wandering about. One of the Golden Girls is in the next booth. A man scoots up to us and introduces himself. 'My name is Winston Young,' he says. 'Young M C.' He raves about 'West End Girls' and 'Opportunities', and how they influenced him.

On the stairs we walk past Joni Mitchell, looking a little drunk, and, quick as a flash, Dainton introduces Neil to her. Neil tells her how much he likes her music, and she seems a little stuck for a reply.

'I like your videos,' she says.

'We do make music too,' he points out.

'I lead such a sheltered life,' she says, and they part.

'She'd had a few,' mutters Neil.

In the hallway Dainton – who, it turns out, has a skill both for recognizing people and introducing them – makes introductions to an actress from *I Dream of Jeannie*, Mickey Dolenz of the Monkees and, most impressively, Steven Spielberg.

'I've been to the Oscars ceremony,' Steven Spielberg tells Neil.

'Well, of course you have,' says Neil.

Neil chats some more with Mickey Dolenz, then we wander out. 'Mickey Dolenz,' he says, 'thought Newcastle was in the Midlands.' He sighs. 'I'm sorry, Steven Spielberg knew who I was . . .'

Tuesday, 26 March

We congregate in reception as gospel soul group the Winans walk past. The mood is sombre. The band members don't quite comprehend what has happened or what its implications might be. They ask Dainton for reassurance that everything is all right, but Dainton simply points out that if Neil and Chris aren't enjoying what they are doing they'll simply end the tour right now.

Neil appears, full of the joys of the Oscar parties. 'I met Steven Spielberg last night,' he tells anyone who'll listen. 'Dainton said, "I want you to meet Neil Tennant of the Pet Shop Boys." It was the "I want" I liked. It was like Dainton was a famous film producer.' He similarly reflects on the encounter with Joni Mitchell: 'I said, "I do make music too." She was a bit pissed, but she looks quite wild, Joni Mitchell. She looks quite untamed by life.' He speculates what might have happened had we bumped into Madonna: 'Dainton would have said, "Madonna, the boys want to work with you. You know you want to work with the boys. When are we going to sit down and do it?"'

'How's Chris?' Sylvia asks him.

'He's all right,' says Neil. Chris is staying in Los Angeles another day to spend time with his parents.

On the aeroplane Neil reads the text of an unofficial Pet Shop Boys book to be called *Introspective*, galleys of which the publishers have sent Neil and Chris to read, presumably to forestall problems later on.

Arma is back and takes Neil out to dinner, Dainton and I in tow. Dainton tells Arma about last night: 'It was one of those evenings when we went out, we gave them "what for?" in Oscarland.'

Neil says he was nearly at the end of his tether after *The Tonight Show*. 'But just at the moment when I've totally had enough and I'm going to leave the group . . .' He sighs, never finishing. 'He never quite goes that far.'

'It's not that hard, as far as I can see, to be Chris,' says Arma, who is still struggling to relate to the situation. 'You travel first class, you make a shit load of money, you do something that has an effect on millions of people and you can basically be yourself. You can't do that in many walks of life . . . ' He sighs. 'This is a real experience with you guys.'

They talk about the problems with EMI, and America.

'A lot of Americans haven't ever bought a Pet Shop Boys record,' says Arma, 'and one day they'll make the plunge and I think it has to be the greatest hits record . . . '

'If one had to talk about the advantages of being on EMI,' says Neil, 'apart from the huge advances they give us . . . we wouldn't be able to talk for long on the subject.'

Arma plans a big showdown with EMI. 'I may lose my temper tomorrow,' he says. 'You don't mind, do you?'

San Francisco Chronicle, 26 March, 'Pet Shop Boys Unleash New Catty Single':
The undertaking is pure Pet Shop Boys. 'We were told, "When you tour America, you simply have to have a live drummer," ' Tennant said, his snappy patter suddenly condescending. 'Therefore, there will be no musicians onstage during our show – it features 10 dancers instead.' The lesson should have been obvious by now. You just can't tell a disco artist what to do.

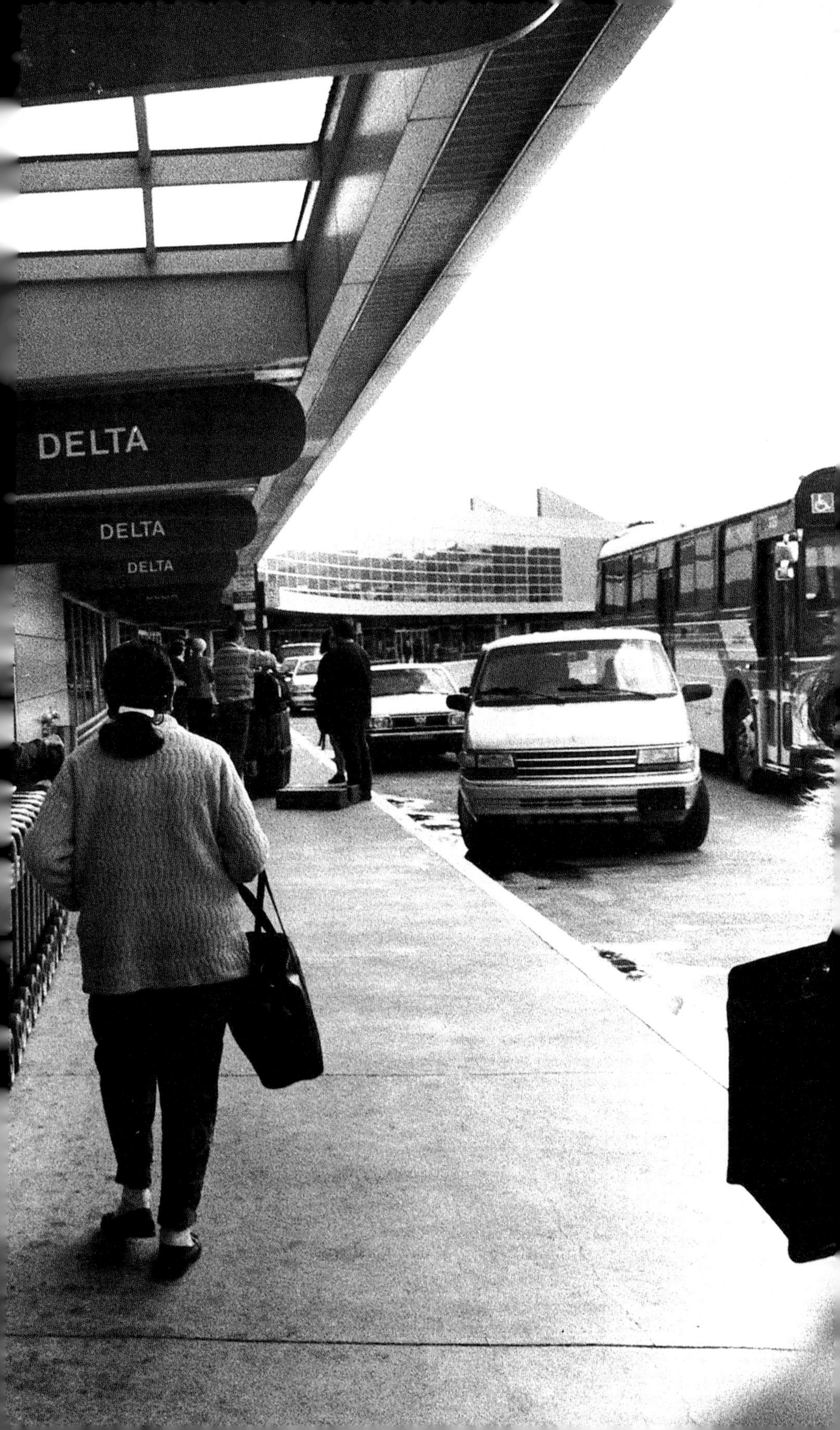
DELTA
DELTA
DELTA

Wednesday, 27 March

On the stage of the Warfield Theater, one of the San Francisco venues owned by promoter Bill Graham, Neil and David Alden stare at the Pet Shop Boys' stage set. It is a tiny stage.

'What am I supposed to be deciding?' asked Neil.

'Nothing really, now you've seen it,' says David Alden.

'So I don't need to stay down here? I might go and buy a pullover.'

Arma greets Chris.

'I hear you raised a little hell in LA,' Arma congratulates Chris. 'I'm proud of you.' Arma saw Chris walk out on TV and thought it must have been part of the act.

'How are Wilson Phillips?' Chris asks Arma.

'They're fine. They're coming to the show, Friday.'

'I hope they bought tickets,' mutters Chris.

Chris asks Richard, the tour accountant, about the projected tour deficit and he suggests '750'.

'750 would be bad,' sighs Chris. 'Three-quarters of a million.'

Ivan overhears this talk. 'There's *no way* it's going to be 750, no way. The things going over can be recharged.'

Chris asks about someone who he thinks is not doing his job well. 'He's getting a right bollocking.'

'He's working for peanuts anyway,' says Ivan, trying to pacify Chris.

'Good,' snaps Chris.

Ivan says that tonight they will click the door, a procedure whereby you physically count everybody who enters the theatre to check whether the numbers declared by the promoter are legitimate.

I go and talk to the fans queuing outside the front of the theatre. The six at the front of the queue have camped overnight to be first in line. 'We've been waiting for years for them to come,' one explains. The queue bunches around and tells me their other favourite bands: Depeche Mode, the Sugarcubes, Erasure, Morrissey. They talk about the Pet Shop Boys.

'They're intelligent pop. They're geniuses.'

'I think they're the best techno pop band there is.'

'They have a pure sense of style. They know art.'

One girl is Dutch: 'I like their – what do you call it? – sarcasm? Their comic approach to serious things.'

'We like both of them because they're different.'

'Naïve.'

'They don't slime like rockers.'

'I've heard the show is very bizarre.'

'Kind of like Pink Floyd.'

'My friends laugh at me for listening to them.'

'A lot of people think they're a silly teenage band like New Kids on the Block.'

'You have to explain that "Shopping" isn't about going to the mall and picking up a new pair of shoes.'

'They think they don't do their own work.'

'They think Neil Tennant sings in a monotone.'

'My parents got so sick of hearing their tape. My dad kind of likes them, but he doesn't admit it. Just recently he said, "I like that, but don't tell anyone."'

Neil and Chris are fretting about how small the theatre is. 'I want to play sheds,' says Chris. Boston is apparently even smaller and Chris suggests cancelling the show there.

'It's the kind of temperamental thing we do,' sighs Neil. 'We're temperamental artists: oh, let's cancel Boston, Detroit, Chicago and Minneapolis!' He pauses. 'Of course San Francisco was the site of the last Sex Pistols concert – I hope that's not significant.'

Chris asks one of the dancers about an amorous episode in Houston.

'I went out to dinner with her,' says the dancer, 'then she went to bed. She had to work.'

'That's typical,' says Chris. 'I hope you've learned your lesson.'

Arma sweeps by. 'So are you enjoying yourself still?' he asks Chris.

'Yup,' says Chris.

'I'm happy about that,' says Arma.

Chris surveys a hand-out that advertises the Pet Shop Boys alongside 'an evening with Yes' and INXS. 'That's one thing I hate about touring, that it puts you on the same page as everyone else.' He looks some more. 'Who's Bootsy Collins?' Someone mutters, 'Funkadelic . . . legend of dance music . . . ' Chris shrugs. 'I don't know anything about dance music.'

Arma discusses the possibility of a party in Los Angeles. It's a tricky city in which to throw a party because everybody drives.

'I'd rather not have a party than have a bad one,' says Chris. 'I wouldn't mind going to a downtown warehouse, but I wouldn't want everybody to come.'

'There's a reception room at the venue that's quite nice,' says Arma. 'I think EMI want to present you with a gigantic cake of the United States.'

They don't like the sound of this, and voice a stream of objections.

'Also,' says Chris, 'neither Neil nor I likes cake, actually. That's another minor problem.'

'Of course,' Neil ruminates, 'they can't give us a gold disc, that's the problem. Maybe they should give us a bronze disc.'

'Are EMI happy?' Pete asks Arma. 'They always had the excuse that the Pet Shop Boys didn't have success because they didn't tour.'

'Well, it's a pretty good excuse,' says Arma. 'Do you ever watch Club MTV?' he asks Neil and Chris, in that tone which means he's tentatively leading up to something.

'Yeah,' says Chris. 'We've done it.'

'Would you do it again?' asks Arma.

'Not now,' says Chris. 'Not now that we're a serious live band.' Pete hits Chris. Arma says that ' . . . Streets . . . ' is doing well in the clubs, then tells Neil that the T-shirt of his face is fifty-three per cent of all sales. The one of Chris, of the back of his head, is lagging behind.

'The crew all wear yours,' Neil points out quite accurately to Chris.

'That's only because I go around telling them off if they're wearing yours,' says Chris.

Ivan comes in. 'We should look at going on at eight o'clock.'

'We're going on at 8.30,' says Neil, who is finishing up a plate of spaghetti. 'I'm just eating my dinner. I'll be burping.'

Ivan persists.

'No!' says Neil. 'I want a little rest.'

Ivan gives up and leaves.

'Ivan didn't get his own way,' comments Chris, surprised. 'We're rock stars. We can go on at ten if we like. That's what it's all about.'

'We should be overdosing in a telephone box in Florida, that's what we should be doing,' says Neil, 'and we should arrive about three hours late when Bill Graham's giving a speech to the audience.'

Dainton fetches Sylvia's humidifier to help Neil's congestion and he sits there, his head in a steam of fumes under a drape.

'Oh, *Neil*,' scolds Chris. 'You're not freebasing? It's like *Blue Velvet . . .*'

David Alden has been wandering around. There is much grief about the compromises made to fit the show into this venue. The backdrop looks terrible. 'Two duvet covers with creases,' as Neil puts it. David Alden ends with the good news. 'There's an incredibly long line for T-shirts,' he says.

'That's what we like to hear,' says Neil. 'Maybe we should just tour the merchandise – we could stand behind the stall and sell it.'

'The old country stars like Johnny Cash would come out in the intervals,' Arma tells them, 'and sell autographs at the stall for ten dollars a shot.'

'This tour should have been sponsored by Nike,' mutters Chris.

'Maybe we could introduce a new concept: retrospective sponsoring.'

'We'll look into that,' laughs Arma. 'You know me – I like commerce.'

There is another row about the sloppiness and compromised nature of the show.

'We're going to have to keep fighting for things,' says David Alden.

'It's getting a bit tedious,' says Chris.

'Even if we tell people it's a very complicated show, it's not *that* complicated,' Neil fumes. 'David Lee Roth flies across the audience. This is a wall with a triangle behind it.'

Arma rushes in, beaming. 'We're moving those T-shirts! They're selling like hot cakes!'

'You mean Neil's are selling like hot cakes,' mopes Chris.

'Chris, you're selling the odd one,' cajoles Neil. 'The sick people buy you.'

'There are people outside trying to get in,' says Arma.

This perks up Chris. 'It's a "hot ticket"! We've finally got one!'

Just before they finally go on Chris lets out a cry of anguish. 'I've forgotten to put my underpants on. My strip . . .'

Tonight, during his strip, he changes the words. Not 'these are the secrets of sexual attraction' but 'these are the secrets of sexual perversion'.

★

The show is a messy success. 'Because it's a shambles,' sighs Neil in the interval, 'it's got more of a light-hearted feel.'

They talk about Chris's strip.

'They're disappointed it doesn't go further,' he says.

'One night you should go further,' suggests Neil. 'That's how you make rock'n'roll history. That's what Jim Morrison did. Not that you see it in the film.'

'That's typical of Hollywood,' grunts Chris. 'They do one interesting thing and it's not in the film.'

They discuss plans to extend the tour to Brazil.

'We ain't flying in a Brazilian plane, I'll tell you that,' announces Neil.

'We can't devote the rest of our lives to touring,' complains Chris.

'Why not?' wonders David Alden.

'Because we're in it to write songs,' says Chris. 'We're in it for the joy of music, not for the money.'

During tonight's encore, just after Neil tells the crowd he loves them, a man in an EMF T-shirt jumps on-stage and hugs Chris, lying on top of him on his bed.

'Where was my security?' asks Chris afterwards, though he is quite clearly thrilled. 'I heard the stage rumbling and then I felt an arm around me and a voice said, "I love you." I'm a professional. I didn't even flinch.'

Arma catches up with us. 'What did you do when that guy jumped on the bed?'

'Nothing,' says Chris. 'What I usually do.'

'Let's face it, he wasn't very attractive,' says Neil. He sighs. 'Usually during "Jealousy" I feel like bursting into tears, but it was pantomime tonight. It's basically *The Rocky Horror Picture Show,* let's face it.'

'There's a couple of fans outside,' says Pete. 'One in a wheelchair.'

'What did he think about the wheelchair bit?' worries Chris.

'He said to me, "Everything they do is brilliant," ' reassures Pete.

Ivan enters. 'Is there a meet'n'greet?' Chris asks him.

'No,' says Ivan.

'No meet'n'greet! What are we meant to *do* for the next twenty minutes?'

Someone tells Chris they must do a T-shirt with his face on.

'No,' he says, 'I'm not for turning.'

★

San Francisco Examiner, *29 March, 'Sensational Pet project':*
When the new world order is firmly established and Madonna becomes president, Neil
Tennant and Chris Lowe – the Pet Shop Boys – will be England's Prime Ministers.
Their Wednesday show . . . was the best, boldest pop spectacle to sweep through the Bay
Area since Madonna's Blond Ambition tour last summer. And like Madonna's staged
extravaganza, this was more performance art than rock concert. This was the future of
pop. It was opera. It was fabulous . . . A man was brought out wrapped up in red cloth
while another sat on a bench like a street person. I think this was supposed to represent
Tennant and Lowe . . . The Pets and the Material Girl draw on similar sources – cabaret,
disco escapism, postmodern deconstruction, religion, sex, camp and the love of a good,
gaudy showstopper followed by another and another. If Madonna fulfilled the dream of
her 'Justify My Love' video and became a male couple, she'd be the Pet Shop Boys.

San Jose Mercury News, *29 March, 'Pet Shop Boys a grandiose treat':*
Finally they're hitting stages with a show that's a cross between a David Lean movie and
a custard pie in the face . . . And like a pie in the face, if it had its embarrassing moments,
it was also fun to lick off . . . the only constants being Tennant and Lowe, who inhabited
the songs as much as performed them . . . 'It's a Sin' unfolded with the Undynamic Duo
dressed up as schoolboys tucked away in a dorm with their classmates, all of whom were
dropping their knickers for wicked masters and cavorting about on beds and such . . . Was
all this a crutch for songs that couldn't stand on their own? Yes and no . . .

Thursday, 28 March

'You can't photograph me today,' announces Chris, breezing into the lobby with Pete. They have been down to Fisherman's Wharf; Pete wanted to see the seals. 'I've just squeezed a massive zit,' Chris explains.

Instead he talks to Pennie about her old subjects, the Clash. He asks where Joe Strummer is now. Making records in his basement. Chris shrugs. 'It's what we're all doing. We've all realized you can make records in your basement for no money and they sound just as good.'

Neil appears, dressed in Romeo Gigli ('Oooh,' coos Chris, 'I should have worn mine'), and they examine today's *San Francisco Examiner*, which shows a still from the 'So Hard' video, the two of them side by side on a Newcastle bus shelter bench.

'I'm always disappointed that there's nothing obscene,' says Neil, meaning in the graffiti behind them in the photo.

'There's something sexy about promenade benches,' says Chris.

Neil suddenly recognizes the name of the *Examiner* writer. 'It's the person who gave *It Couldn't Happen Here* a good review!'

'We shouldn't meet him,' counsels Chris. 'It's always bad to meet people who like you, because they're always mega-disappointed.'

It is now that Neil chooses to impart a health bulletin. 'I'm seriously ill, everyone.' Pause. 'But, of course, the show must go on.'

'Lucky the show's all on tape,' says Chris.

We are due at a local radio station, Live 105, but the EMI representative is late to pick us up. 'Why did we re-sign to EMI?' grunts Chris.

'Because they gave us a lot of money,' says Neil.

'Money isn't everything,' says Chris.

'No,' says Neil, pointedly referring the notion back to Chris, 'it isn't.'

Still no EMI man.

'Let's get a cab!' suggests Chris. '*That'll* embarrass him.' This idea fills him with enthusiasm. 'Let's go now. Before he has a chance to come.'

In the cab they discuss media requests: a *Good Morning America* interview (no – too early in the morning); a Lynn Goldsmith photo session (maybe); an *Entertainment Tonight* TV interview (yes, if under their terms). Neil tells Chris the new British '... Streets ...' chart news. Last Sunday it was number four. This week it is predicted to be number six.

'At least it went up last week,' mutters Chris.

'I've realized,' Neil sighs, 'I don't think we'll ever have a huge hit again.'

We pull up outside an anonymous block-shaped building.

'We've been here before,' says Neil.

Inside, the DJ starts raving about their tour as soon as he spots Neil and Chris; his partner, who actually saw the show, even more so. 'I thought I was at a Broadway show,' the partner gushes.

'Good,' says Chris. 'That's what we wanted.'

They are asked about their U2 cover version. In San Francisco, the DJ tells them, this is An Issue.

'Why did you do it?' he asks.

'I don't know why we did it,' answers Chris.

'It was your idea,' Neil points out.

'I don't remember,' says Chris. Pause. 'It was a homage to U2.'

The DJ pauses, both to digest this and to see whether Chris's deadpan expression cracks. It doesn't.

'So why "Can't Take My Eyes Off You"?' the DJ continues uncertainly.

'It just seemed the obvious thing to do,' says Chris.

They are asked to choose one of their own songs – Neil suggests the single version of 'Left to My Own Devices' – and while it is playing the DJ tells them that he and his partner will be DJ-ing at their aftershow appearance that night at the Palladium. It is a tricky moment.

'We don't know about it,' says Chris. This is true.

'This is a *planned promotion*,' says the DJ, desperation already flooding his voice, his hope seeming to be that this phrase 'planned promotion' will ring some bells. The man from EMI, who has belatedly arrived, makes a cack-handed attempt to paper over the cracks by saying, 'We're going to a lot of clubs.'

Neil stares right at him, daggers. 'We've a bus-ride right after the show.' There follows an argument between the man from EMI (cocksure but out of his depth) and the DJ (all heartfelt injustice).

'We've been *promoting* it.'

'It wasn't set for *sure.*'

'It was set for *sure* sure.'

'This,' interjects Neil, 'is *literally* the first we have heard of it.'

The EMI man leaves the room. Chris gestures at the air he occupied. 'This guy is ...' and he makes a face to convey his contempt. Then the on-air interview begins. The DJ asks if they feel 'shackled' by their American record label.

'I sometimes think there's not enough shackling,' says Neil. 'There's no shackling at all. It works like a large independent. You just give them the record and they put it out. On EMI you stand or fall by what you do; they put it in the shops.'

The DJ asks Neil about Electronic, closing with an inquiry as to their album title.

'*Electronic,*' says Neil.

'Wow!' exclaims the DJ. 'It's *Meet the Beatles!*'

While the next record plays – they request the KLF's 'What Time is Love?' – they tell the DJ they will turn up at the club tonight anyway, at about 11.00 p.m., on the way to Los Angeles. They sign some posters as competition prizes, Neil inscribing each of them with today's date. 'This is the new pretentious thing we do,' he explains.

In the car they fret about the chore they've taken on.

'After about an hour,' Chris sighs theatrically, 'and after rather a lot to drink, we'll leave. Because actually' – a grin slips through – 'we love doing it. People coming up to us, telling us we're "awesome" ... '

Back at the hotel Chris phones his room and Dainton answers.

'Can you be a bit more polite,' scolds Chris, 'when answering my phone?'

5.30 p.m. Arma is giving the tour accountant, Richard, a pep talk. His current subject: American concert promoters.

'We're giving these guys a taste. We're giving them a nice inexpensive introduction to the Pet Shop Boys. Then we clobber them in the fall.' His voice crescendos. 'Suck 'em in, blow 'em out – that's what I say.'

Neil is still ailing. 'I feel shit,' he moans. 'I've got flu.'

'Well,' says Chris, 'I don't know if you can go on the bus with me – all those germs in that confined space. Didn't you buy a mesh in Japan?' Neil just looks at him. 'Cheer up, Neil,' adds Chris.

'You can bloody talk,' grumps Neil. 'That's why we have a miserable image, because *you're* so miserable.'

'Yes,' agrees Chris, 'but it's not an image – '

Ivan interrupts to say that the New York hotel is booked. It's Chris's choice, the Philippe Starck-designed Royalton. They've given a good rate but have refused to allow the tour bus to pull up outside. 'They just don't like the idea,' says Ivan.

Arma relates his growing frustrations with EMI. 'I got crazy with them today,' he says.

'They're never going to have a better chance than this,' sighs Chris.

'I'm going to go so wild,' Arma sighs. 'If they want an arsehole manager screaming at them they're going to get one.'

They discuss the New York party which is being planned by night-life socialite Kiki Mason. As he is with all party arrangements, Chris is worried. 'We've got to get in touch with Kiki.' He makes a face. 'He wants boy go-go dancers...'

'... with wings on,' sighs Neil.

'Who's that?' asks Arma.

'This Kiki bloke,' says Chris.

'Kiki,' asks Arma, 'or kinky?'

'Both,' says Neil.

'It sounds as though I might not like this party,' Chris pronounces. 'Kiki said, "Obviously it'll have a heavy gay ambience..."'

This isn't what they want.

'I did tell him "more hispanic than gay",' says Neil.

'I want it dangerous,' says Chris. 'I want gangs there.'

'All New York parties are the same,' sighs Neil with resignation.

'I wonder if there'll be a metal detector when you walk in,' says Chris. 'I like that.'

Arma wants to think about tomorrow night after the first Los Angeles show. 'Afterwards, even if we haven't got anything planned, we should do something spontaneously.'

Chris glances at him, and answers, all the sarcasm buried, 'Let's plan to do something spontaneous.'

In the dressing-room Neil flicks through a copy of *Camera International*. 'It's a well-known fact,' he declares, 'that all photography magazines have a

male nude in. Where is it?' Flicks. 'First male nude,' he announces triumphantly. Flicks on. 'Second male nude ... third male nude ... fourth male
nude ...'

Robbie comes to brief them about the technical shortcomings of tonight's
show and they – Robbie, Neil, Chris and David Alden – have a long, sometimes
heated discussion about the continued shoddiness of the backdrop and the lack
of snow. Finally Chris exclaims, sulkily and with gloriously impractical hindsight,
'What we should be using is yachting technology. Yachts are just tension. I bet
it's dead simple.' When Robbie leaves the room David Alden pulls a copy of
Rolling Stone over his face and pretends to cry.

Next they tease Dainton over the worth of cockney rhyming slang. 'I've
never understood the point of it,' huffs Neil.

Dainton enthusiastically demonstrates. 'I'll say, "He's talking pony", and
that's "rubbish".' Pony trap. Crap.

'I'd rather people said "rubbish",' mutters Chris.

'The only cockney rhyming slang I've ever liked is Lionels – "Lionel Blairs"
for "flares",' says Neil. 'It's almost worth it for that.'

It is almost showtime. 'I'm sure I might manage to stagger through,' hams
Neil, 'even though I'm *desperately* ill.'

'I think we should call our greatest hits *Awesome*, or *Rad*,' says Chris as they
walk towards the stage. 'It should be very America. Maybe we should just make
the sleeve the American flag.' Pause. 'You know, if I was the Edge I'd send lots
of postcards, and call them Postcards from the Edge.'

The concert is a delight, the audience packed up against the stage,
screaming. 'It's a natural high,' Neil declares in the interval. He tells us how
tonight Catherine ate the rose with which she frolics: 'She said, "I'm a method
actress."'

'A methadone actress,' mutters David Alden, more because it sounds
good than for any other reason. 'God, it's a mess, 'but I'm getting not to
care.'

'Luckily we can get away with murder,' laughs Neil.

'Four minutes!' Howard hollers.

'I need a few more,' Chris complains. 'Think of the merchandising.'

During the encore a man gets up on-stage and kisses Neil. Neil pats him
on the shoulder. Then, once Neil is lying down at the end of 'Your Funny
Uncle', another man jumps up and asks him to sign an autograph. He does. 'It
seemed churlish,' he recounts later, 'not to.'

★

On the bus:

'This *is* an adventure,' says a rather thrilled Arma, 'getting on this bus, camping out with the Pet Shop Boys.'

'I've got an idea for the greatest hits,' says Chris. '*Seven Marvellous Years.*'

'It should be sexy,' corrects Neil. '*Seven Sexy Years,* or something.'

We stop, as promised, at the Palladium. At the entrance, by the bouncers, is a photocopy of the *Behaviour* sleeve photograph, next to which is the message 'These are what the Pet Shop Boys look like . . . study this photo carefully.'

Neil and Chris take over the turntables and play a few records. One of the radio DJs confesses to them that he is a musician too and gives them some copies of the single he has made, which they promise to give a listen. Neil hands the records to me, reckoning I won't lose them. I put them down, get drunk, and forget all about them. Nobody ever asks me what happened to them.

After a while we pile on to the bus and settle down for the overnight drive to Los Angeles. Chris looks perplexed. He has a problem. 'I never know how to get rid of chewing-gum,' he says. 'That's why I never accept it.'

Entertainment Weekly, *19 April, 'Where the Pet Shop Boys Are':*

Until last year, the Pet Shop Boys shunned performing live. And you could see why at their March 28 show at the Warfield Theater in San Francisco . . . The shy duo prefers to rely on their wits rather than their charisma – and wits are pretty hard to visualize . . . The audience was treated to a shifting array of futuristic images – like the giant cloud-filled window and exploding clock that dominated the stage – culled from paintings by such surrealists as Salvador Dali and René Magritte. There were many other references to arty authors, painters and movies . . . It wasn't until the encore (. . . 'Always on My Mind' . . .) that the band first cracked a smile – and, incidentally, that the audience began to cheer, clap and dance along, acting, at last, as if they were at a concert or discotheque rather than at a pretentious art salon surrounded by snooty aesthetes.

Friday, 29 March

Neil is thinking about the future. 'According to my pension plan,' he mutters, 'I retire at forty-five. Only nine years to go . . .'

Someone observes that he'll be like Malcolm Muggeridge.

'Yes,' he sighs. 'I'll be incredibly right wing, or left wing, or very religious, or a complete atheist. Someone said, "Anyone who knows something very well is invariably right wing about it." I'm not saying that's right, but all the teachers I know, they all voted for comprehensives and now they hate it.' Pause. 'I'm thinking of becoming a communist now. I love lost causes.'

Arma appears. 'That guy at the club last night was so grateful,' he grins. 'I don't think we'll have a problem with airplay on that station for a couple of years.'

Chris is worrying about tonight. 'This is the one they're all saying will be really good' – the Pet Shop Boys have been popular in Los Angeles since the release of the Bobby 'O' version of 'West End Girls' – 'so it'll probably be a disaster.'

We drive to the Universal Amphitheater: me, Neil, Chris, Arma, Neil's brother Philip and his girlfriend. The traffic is bad. 'A lot of people are scrambling to get home before Passover,' says Arma. 'You have to be home before sundown.'

'Does that mean no one's coming to the concert?' asks Chris.

'I think there'll be six thousand gentiles,' says Arma.

'So are they indoors all the time?' asks Philip.

'No,' says Arma. 'Houston was outdoors.'

'I think he means the Jews,' Chris points out.

'Oh,' says Arma. 'I don't know. I'm Episcopalian.'

Chris teases Neil by saying, about Philip, 'He's got a different accent to you. He sounds like a Geordie.'

'I *have* lived in London for eighteen years,' says Neil in his most imperious voice, then laughs. 'Not that I sound any different from when I first arrived.'

'You don't say "white water rafting" anyway,' says Philip, pronouncing 'rafting' as a posh southerner might.

'Simon's got this video,' Neil explains – Simon is their other brother – 'of him in the Zambezi. We all take the piss out of him saying "white water rafting". We think he's gone colonial.'

'He's coming back soon, isn't he?' says Chris.

'September,' says Neil.

Chris considers this for a few seconds, the return from Africa. 'I'd miss the staff,' he says. We drive on. 'Have you ever seen a satellite picture of LA?' asks Chris. 'It looks really good. Just grids.'

We pass Hollywood High School.

'Is Hollywood High a good school?' Neil asks Arma.

'No. Not somewhere I'd send my kids to. The Beverly Hills High School, maybe.' He tells us that the parking lot of the latter is split into two halves. 'The teachers have Toyotas and Volkswagens; the kids have Ferraris and Porsches.'

Backstage Chris talks about vomiting: 'I can't drink cider. Or Martini. When I was younger I used to spend all Friday night throwing up in a bin. It was really crap. I had a friend who could drink more, and they expected you to keep up.'

The surprising news circulates that Axl Rose has asked for tickets for tonight's concert.

'I bet he doesn't come,' says Neil, then adds, 'though, let's face it, there's not a lot to do in LA. It's a bit like being in Milton Keynes.'

They do some interviews. Richard Blade from the local radio station KROQ asks them things like 'How do you feel about two sold-out nights tonight?' and then they are filmed for *Entertainment Tonight*. Chris tells them that the audiences have been 'way over the top – in San Francisco they kept jumping on the stage and kissing us'. He explains the show: 'We play the Pet Shop Boys, or at least a strange form of the Pet Shop Boys, and they try to kill us and we die and we go to heaven'. Neil says that the pigs in 'Opportunities' are 'meant, I think, to represent people in the music business'. Then the interviewer asks about the book *Pet Shop Boys, Literally* and Neil gestures towards me, crouching off camera taking notes.

'In fact, he's doing a new one,' says Neil. 'You're in Chapter 6.'

I watch Chris watching the dancers exercising, lifting their legs over their heads.

'It annoys me they can do that and I can't,' he says. 'I hate people who are good at everything. There is always one at school – good at sports, really brainy, and they end up at Oxford.' Pause. 'But they always screw up in the end.'

Back in the dressing-room Pete lampoons their death scene finale.

'We get no respect,' grunts Neil. 'I don't know how we put up with it. We take them on the world tour and we don't get any respect.' Pause. 'Except for some of the dancers, and then only when they want something.'

Chris's parents arrive. Mrs Lowe is full of gossip she has overheard at her hotel about Gary Kemp's new film.

'This is David Alden,' introduces Chris, 'who directed the show, so if you have any complaints it's him you can complain to. I'm just following orders.'

'How are your parents, Neil?' inquires Mr Lowe. 'Playing golf?'

'Yes,' nods Neil. 'They're coming to see the show in Berlin. They want to see the Berlin Wall.'

'It's not there any more,' pipes Chris. 'Don't they know?'

Chris parades his hairstyle: 'I've deliberately not cut it until after you've gone.'

Pete tells them about the fan kissing Chris on-stage in San Francisco.

'What did you do?' asks Mrs Lowe.

'I'm a professional,' Chris smirks. 'The show must go on.'

'No comment,' says Mrs Lowe, clearly remembering *The Tonight Show.* 'No comment.'

'You should be going now,' says Chris.

'He doesn't hint,' chuckles Neil.

They go.

'Your parents look well,' comments Neil.

'They're happy,' shrugs Chris.

'You take after your father quite a lot, don't you?' Neil continues. 'He's a bit of a nervous wreck too. I could imagine them living here. Blackpool and America are quite similar. It's a kind of attitude. Blackpool thinks of itself as an entertainment town.'

'Well, it is,' says Chris.

A hanger-on whom they met on a previous trip is hanging on outside.

'He said to me one of my favourite things anyone's ever said to me in America,' says Neil. ' "Have you heard of Levi's?" '

The endless debate over their career starts over again.

'All we've got to do now,' Chris announces, 'is make a really good record.'

'Yes,' concurs Neil. 'I think we shouldn't release the greatest hits album until we have a sensational record. But I think maybe after this tour we might come up with something a little bit fabulous.'

The discussion winds on for some minutes.

'We've gone off the boil with the public,' sighs Neil. 'We'll sell out three Wembleys with a bit of a struggle.'

'It's all down to the album not being as good,' says Chris.

'I think we've lost some of the teenage audience,' digresses Neil.

'I think we've got to write some simpler, hooky music,' says Chris.

'Yeah,' says Neil. 'That's what I think.'

'I think we've disappeared up our own backsides,' says Chris.

'No,' halts Neil, 'I don't think that.'

'I think we have. Lyrically.' Pause. 'Not just that. We don't write anything simple any more, like "Let's Make Lots of Money".'

Brad, who is from their American booking agency, is chatting in the corridor.

'A friend of mine went to see the show in San Francisco. He described it as like a Magritte painting on acid.'

Inside they are nearly ready.

'Isn't it exciting?' says Neil.

'I only look forward to the end,' says Chris.

'I like the end too,' agrees Neil, 'because you can sort of give in and look at the audience.' He smiles. 'It's kind of a professional night tonight. They're doing it in Hollywood! It takes a bit of a nerve.'

'This could be the night,' taunts Chris, 'when the computer crashes.'

Neil is furious. 'Don't say that! Don't say that! Don't say that!'

'Yesterday,' says Chris, sidestepping Neil's annoyance, 'I made the mistake of drinking lots of water, and midway through the first song I thought uh-oh . . . '

'Chris,' sighs Neil, 'has got a notoriously weak bladder.'

As they walk to the stage Arma tells them, beaming, 'This is the show we were told not to do.' Their booking agents told them they should be booked into a two-thousand-seat venue for one night only in Los Angeles, but their pride couldn't accept that they weren't a bigger draw than that. Instead they booked one, then two, shows at the six-thousand-seater Universal Amphitheater and have sold them out.

'We have got,' nods Neil, 'a right to gloat.'

★

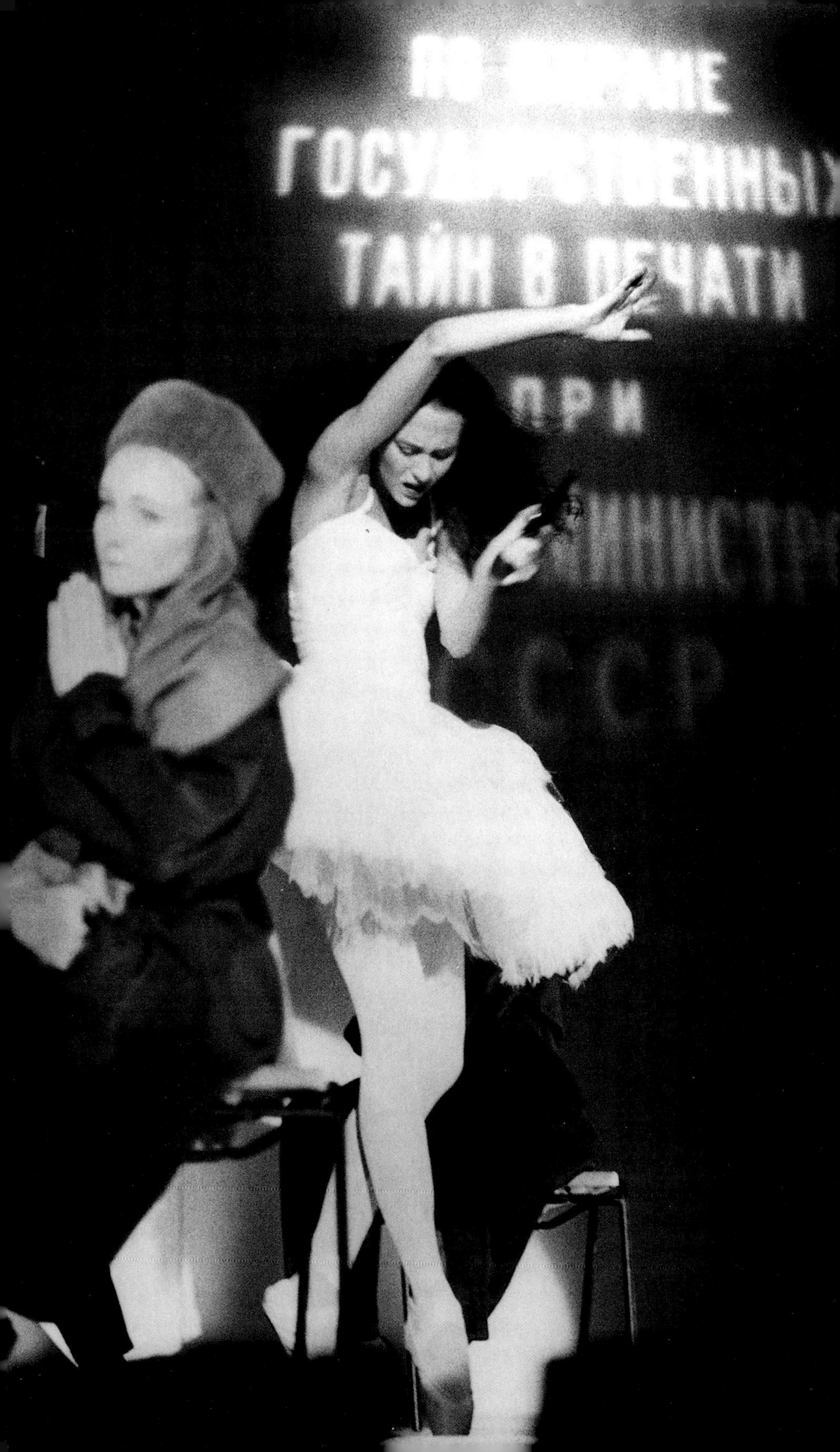
ТАЙН В ПЕЧАТИ

Halftime. The audience has seemed a little baffled by the first half.

'After the lights went on,' says Arma (meaning the interval lights), 'they were all thinking, what was *that*?'

'Good,' says Chris, 'because they're going to have a quiz afterwards.' He complains that he spotted Craig grinning as he split apart Stalin's head with a hammer and sickle. 'I think he doesn't realize that some of us are quite sad about the demise of communism.'

Ivan sweeps in, shaking his head with a smile, as if to say, what *is* this town? 'People were coming up to me after thirty seconds going, "It's a great show!" I said, "How do you know?" '

In the dressing-room, afterwards, sits a cake in the shape of America, courtesy of EMI.

'We're not having pictures of us with a cake all across the trade papers,' snaps Chris immediately.

'Arma,' agrees Neil, 'no photos with the cake. We'll do a photo with the EMI people, no problem. No photo with the cake. We'll do the photos, and we'll pretend the cake never happened.'

'It's not even a cake of America,' Chris complains. 'It looks more like Puerto Rico.'

'Can I talk about the cake here?' says Arma. He is in trouble, struggling. 'I think the concept of the cake is a symbolic one. You're conquering America.'

'With the help of EMI,' sniggers Chris.

Arma leaves to do some schmoozing. Ivan walks in. How well he knows them. Before anyone says anything he says, 'I'm not talking about the cake.'

'It's completely Spinal Tap,' says Chris. Pause. 'It's a matter of *principle*. We're not cake-eaters.'

Arma returns. 'I've got a wild card for you. This *is* Spinal Tap. Axl Rose . . . '

' . . . wants to be photographed with the cake?' asks Chris.

'He's *here*,' says Arma.

'He stayed to the end?' says Chris. 'Why would he want to do that? Hey! Fancy Axl Rose wanting to be photographed with tragic old us.'

They prepare to meet the gathering in the hospitality area. They have been drinking champagne in the dressing-room out of the Pepsi cups provided, but as they are now stepping out into public they search for, and find, some logo-free vessels and decant their drinks. Outside – to the sound of Erasure, which is someone's idea of suitable music for a Pet Shop Boys party – they walk straight

into Axl Rose, who turns out to be unfailingly friendly and sweet. They had assumed that he couldn't have known much about them, but the first thing he says is, 'Gorgeous show – why didn't you do "Being Boring"?' After they have chatted and had their photo taken – one will end up in *Rolling Stone* – I talk to Axl a while. He tells me he asked for four tickets, but couldn't get any of his friends to come with him. 'One finally did, and said, "They don't know what they're missing."'

I express some surprise at finding him here.

'I used to hate them,' he allows. 'I was the guy at the MTV awards who shouted out, "The Pet Shop Boys suck!"' At first I assume this allusion is metaphorical, but then I realize he means it quite literally. The Pet Shop Boys played at the MTV awards in 1986. 'I shouted out during a quiet bit when they played "West End Girls". But when I really hate someone I get all their records to try and work out why, and I found I really like them.'

He proceeds to rave about the show – 'that was so cool, "My October Symphony", when they don't even sing' – and says that liking them is becoming a shared secret in his world. 'I phoned up the singer of Nine Inch Nails and I said, "What's that you're listening to?" and he said, "Oh, er, it's the Pet Shop Boys."' He tells me he plays *Behaviour* in the car and his friends say, 'What are you trying to make me like *now* . . . ?' Then he tells me that there's something in common between 'My October Symphony' and this song he's struggling with in the studio at the moment, a song called 'November Rain'. But his favourite song on *Behaviour* is 'Being Boring'. 'That bit about the seventies and the nineties. I can certainly relate to that, because I left home too . . .'

Back in the dressing-room Neil and Chris compare notes.

'*Well*, Axl Rose,' says Neil. 'He was the one who shocked me. But he's seen the light. He told me that when they were recording their album, during the breaks they'd listen to *Behaviour*, and he said we were an inspiration to them.'

Neil's friend from the other night, Young MC, was there too. Neil wonders belatedly about a problem of etiquette.

'Is it correct to call Young MC "Young"?' he wonders. 'I said, "Nice to see you, Young."'

'Did you speak to the Lowes?' asks Philip. 'She said it was very good. He said it was "different".'

But tonight they are happy.

'You know,' says Neil, 'it's quite a good idea not touring for five years after your first hit, because just when people are going off the boil it kind of revitalizes you.'

Los Angeles Times, *1 April, 'Rock-Theater Revival'*:
For all the knowing edges and satirical thrusts of their tart social commentaries about class, art, consumption and sex, the Pet Shop Boys managed to generate a sympathy – not for themselves as stars, certainly, and not even as stage characters, but for the confusing, sad world whose poets they've become.

Saturday, 30 March

Chris returns from one of his favourite Los Angeles spots, the Hollywood Diner. 'They still have our picture up,' he says, his tone a mixture of surprise and pride. 'I thought they'd have taken it down.' He likes it here. 'A life by the pool is right up my street. The only thing I'd miss is the pop music. I'd have to get the latest records flown in every week.'

Neil has just met Depeche Mode singer Dave Gahan on the Mondrian Hotel terrace having what Neil calls 'a bit of a spooky lunch' with Ivan. 'He said, "I'm really trying to get away from rock'n'roll at the moment." I thought, oh, that's why you've moved to Hollywood, then. He's got a Dave Stewart beard.'

'I'm not surprised he lives here,' Chris chips in. 'Where would you rather live – LA or Basildon?'

'Basildon,' mutters Neil.

They discuss staying in Los Angeles one day longer than scheduled and then, instead of taking the bus overnight to Salt Lake City, flying the next morning.

'It's better to be here,' argues Chris. 'You might be turned on by that whole religious thing.'

'Mormons don't take on Catholics,' says Neil. 'They used to come round and we'd say we were Catholic and they'd just go away.'

'Wasn't Axel F nice?' says Chris, changing the subject. 'I couldn't believe how nice he was.'

'He said it was "fuckin' gorgeous, man"!' says Neil. ' "Fuckin' gorgeous"!'

Chris turns to Arma: 'Morrissey's got a big billboard outside Tower Records. It's annoying, seeing his on the front and ours four rows down. I find billboards more important than anything else.'

'The windows cost maybe five to six thousand dollars,' explains Arma, 'but they're not doing that without Tower doing a deal. Record companies rarely take advertising just for imaging – it's usually tied into an account.'

Neil remembers something and laughs. 'I got a call last night,' he says.

'They said, "Is that the Pet Shop Boys?" and I said, "No, they're in 1121." ' He laughs. Chris's room. Except . . .

'I'm not in 1121,' says Chris. 'I'm in 1021.'

'Oh dear.'

At the Universal Amphitheater:

'You look like Freddie Kruger,' Trevor tells Chris.

'So *he* goes to Michiko in London, does he?' asks Chris.

Neil studies a newspaper article. ' "Deadpan vocals",' sighs Neil. It's the phrase that pops up again and again in their reviews. 'I'd happily never hear that again.'

'At least you don't get the Al Stewart thing any more,' says Chris.

Neil sees me write this down. 'Except in this book,' he complains.

Now Chris sighs. 'You know,' he says, 'I think I prefer the meet'n'greet to the actual show.'

Neil opens a letter. It's from an actor called Bryan Lawrence who writes that he worked with them when they filmed 'Always on My Mind' for a TV tribute to Elvis Presley, *Love Me Tender* – 'I was a mere hand-jiver in the chorus' – and now has a play opening in Los Angeles.

Lynn Goldsmith arrives to take their photo. They are dressed as schoolboys for the first song.

'Is that a hat in your pocket?' she asks Chris. 'I thought you had a strange fetish.'

'I do . . . ' says Chris.

' . . . but that's not it,' completes Neil.

On the way upstairs to do the photos we pass Carnie Wilson from Wilson Phillips, picking from a tray in a hospitality room.

'I still maintain it's good she's fat,' says Neil. 'Who was more famous – Mama Cass or Michelle Phillips?'

Ivan tells them that tonight's show is a complete sell-out. A hundred ticketless fans are outside. 'If George Michael walked up now there's nothing I could do for him. "George, there's no room at the inn. There's a cowshed down the road." '

During the halfway break Janet Street-Porter and her boyfriend TV presenter Normski come backstage, and she boasts how she has been shouting at over-enthusiastic fans in front of them to sit down.

Pete takes a Polaroid of everyone.

After the show Neil walks into the dressing-room and his wings fall off. 'I'm too sweaty, I haven't got my hat, my wings have come off,' he sighs. 'It's all too late.'

'It's all falling apart,' says Chris.

Janet tells a story of going to the Roxbury with a famous rock manager: Terence Trent D'Arby and Lenny Kravitz came over to their table and he said, as they approached, 'Look, girls! It's Milli Vanilli!'

There are separate limos back to the hotel. I pile into Neil's.

'We got away with it again,' he smiles a little drunkenly, and starts singing '*I've been getting away with it . . .*'. He mentions that when Janet saw the show's dress rehearsal at the Brixton Academy early in the month she had said, 'That's all your fans between fourteen and twenty-two killed off.'

Ivan asks Neil whether – as he declared early on during the last tour – he has begun to think about what he'll be having for dinner afterwards while on-stage.

'No,' he says, 'I've got too much to do in this show.' Pause. 'Also, I have dinner beforehand.'

Deseret News, *Salt Lake City, 30 March, 'Pet Shop Boys performing Monday'*: *No fooling, come April 1st another invasion will take place, only this time in Salt Lake City. And there's no general leading the attack by the name of Schwarzkopf. True, America's most loyal ally, Great Britain, is once again sending her sons into the fray, although this invasion has nothing to do with guns or butter, for that matter. At least not the kind of butter you spread on toast . . .*

Sunday, 31 March

Janet Street-Porter and Normski are staying in a house on Malibu beach owned by Steve Fargnoli (until recently one of Prince's managers, now manager of Sinead O'Connor, among others). They have invited Neil for lunch and so Dainton drives him along Sunset Boulevard and then up the coast, Pennie and myself in tow.

We sit round and enjoy a drink and the view. This small strip is where the Hollywood and music millionaires live. Robert de Niro's house is a couple along. 'I thought I might see them all beach-stepping,' says Normski, 'but they're all polishing their Grammies and Oscars.'

Normski puts on a record by Another Bad Creation and Neil reminisces about listening to Led Zeppelin's 'Stairway to Heaven' – final line 'she's buying a stairway to heaven' – when he was younger.

'I always thought it was about shopping for a Stairway to Heaven,' he says. 'I always had this vision of a woman going to Peter Jones in Sloane Square and saying, "Do you have a Stairway to Heaven?" . . . "No, I wanted one in blue . . . " '

Neil is still feeling a little under the weather and he is directed towards a cupboard where a previous house visitor, Sinead O'Connor, has left half a packet of a pick-me-up called Wow! He tries a sachet and it works a treat, so he is encouraged to take the remains of Sinead's supply.

He frets about American insularity. 'I tried to phone up Zambia and the hotel operator had never heard of it. She said, "Do you want the code for Africa?" They're not absolutely convinced the rest of the world exists.' Someone drinks a glass of orange juice. 'Orange juice,' he pronounces, 'can give you stomach cancer. There are diseases in California because people drink too much orange juice.' Pause. 'Actually, I might have just made that up.'

Normski appears with his new hat, a floppy gold and black creation like an upside-down pyramid. We all try it on. He's already been told it looks like it's by Rifat Ozbek. Neil says it's very early Michael Jackson.

'I'm glad you said that,' says Normski, 'because you just lowered your credibility below the belt, baby. I bought it on Venice beach.'

We take a walk along the beach. It is deserted.

'Right!' snaps Neil. 'Where's Madonna, then? Where's Madonna, Sting, Robert de Niro and Jack Nicholson?' As yet, there is no one. 'Of course,' he adds, 'if we see them, we'll pretend we don't recognize them . . .'

Monday, 1 April

On the way to the airport:

'You've got the sun,' Pennie tells Chris.

'I used a suntanning cream,' says Chris.

Neil reads a review. It is positive, but he is not impressed. 'This is what I call a "despite . . ." review. Despite the fact they've got no personalities, despite the fact he can't sing, despite the fact they're ironic . . .'

Chris reads it. 'They're all here,' he sighs. ' "Deadpan" . . . "ironic" . . .'

'The usual words,' sighs Neil.

'We could have a checklist,' Chris suggests.

'They've gorra lorra lorra irony,' mutters Neil.

The two of them complain about the paparazzi. EMI are always inviting them when they're not welcome. 'Last year at the record signing,' says Neil, 'we threw them out and they were all shouting, "Hope your record does shit." '

'We're just surrounded by hopeless people,' says Chris.

We arrive at the airport.

'We're flying Delta, are we?' asks Chris. 'The airline that serves food. That's how I would advertise if I was them: "We serve food." '

Inside the terminal he spots a marine and decides he wants his photo taken with him. 'Welcome home, our boys,' he says deadpan.

'He looks a bit tired,' Neil points out. 'He doesn't quite look ready for a photo opportunity.'

But he is.

'You in a band?' he asks Chris.

'Yes. The Pet Shop Boys.'

'Oh yeah?'

They talk a while, then Chris returns. 'He just came back from "the war effort",' Chris tells us.

'How was it for him?' inquires Neil.

'Great,' says Chris. 'He kicked Iraqi ass.'

We chat about the war. Whenever we talk about the Gulf War Neil calls

Schwarzkopf Schwarzenegger. Then, as we sit here, a whole group of marines disembark and kids run up to them, waving flags. 'Hey!' shouts one of them, 'He's home!' and nearly everyone in the airport lounge applauds.

'Have you noticed?' comments Neil quietly. 'They all do what they do on television.' Pause. 'If I'd been at war for five years, and been in the jungle, my father would meet me at the airport and shake my hand, and we'd drive home probably more or less in silence.' And – his tone conveys – a fine, sensible state of affairs that would be.

We watch some more. One of the marines is literally leapt upon by an adoring friend.

'Oh,' sighs Chris, 'actually that's pretty genuine, that is. We're just too cynical.'

Salt Lake City Airport:

'You know,' says Chris, 'Mormons look pretty much like anybody else.'

The city is set on a plain surrounded by a distant ring of snow-capped mountains.

'I'm not very impressed by mountains,' says Chris. 'That whole Switzerland thing. They just look like chocolate boxes. They've never done anything for me. That's why I like LA so much, because the mountains in the distance aren't *corny* ones. It's "snow-capped mountains" I hate.'

We are met by Steve from EMI, still talking about Queensryche, who fills us in on the liquor laws: no liquor shop sales on Sundays, no doubles ever. Until the Winter Olympics were held here you couldn't buy spirits with a mixer.

'I can imagine things happen in this town,' says Chris with relish. 'Unexpected things.'

The man from EMI enthusiastically tells us that Eric Burdon and Brian Auger are playing in a local club late tonight.

'I'm sorry,' says Neil, to widespread derision, 'I'm going to see Eric Burdon! He's one of the original Geordies.' (He doesn't, of course.)

Before going to the hotel there is a radio station stop, at HOT 94.9 KZHT. The men from EMI grovel to the programme director's young daughter, Ricki, as though she were the most important person in Utah. To them, maybe, she is.

'Would you guys like anything to drink?' asks the programme director. 'Ovaltine perhaps?' Laughs. It's a the-English-are-in-town joke.

'I've never had Ovaltine in my life,' mutters Neil.

We sit with the DJ waiting for the commercials to finish. Hair care.

Weddings. Mexican food. During the last one the DJ says, to us but not to his listeners, 'I just had some, and I feel like puking now.' The next ad is for pizza. 'Do you like pizza?' the ad inquires. 'No,' says the DJ, 'I hate pizza.'

The interview is dull but pleasant. It ends like this:

'Before I let you go, which one of you worked in the Pet Shop?'

'Oh, neither of us,' says Chris. 'A friend did.'

'Oh! I like it!'

Outside the studio a girl fan rushes up to them. 'You're Lowe!' she exclaims to Chris.

'That's my last name,' he confirms evenly.

'I'm Lowe too,' she explains, clearly quite overcome by the coincidence.

They are dragged away to do some station IDs. Neil gets confused midway. 'Hi,' he says, 'I'm Chris ... Oh. I'm not, actually.'

The fans are still there when Neil and Chris have finished. They have lots of expensive import copies of the Pet Shop Boys' records. They ask Neil and Chris to sign a copy of the original 'Opportunities', which still carries a $34.99 price sticker. There's a local shop, they explain, which sells this stuff. Or, rather, did. 'They closed down last week.'

'That's the curse of the Pet Shop Boys,' says Neil.

The EMI man asks them to write an autograph for someone by the name of Elder Warner. 'He's a missionary,' the EMI man explains.

'He wants *our* autograph?' says Neil. 'What kind of a missionary is he?'

We drive into town.

'We haven't,' Neil complains, 'met one of the Osmonds yet.'

We wander round the town on foot. As we pass the Mormon Family History Museum we debate whether it's true that we're all already listed in there, waiting to be claimed retrospectively (when you convert, your ancestors come with you) to the Mormon faith. Chris takes a photo of a fake log cabin. A sign says 'Erected 1983–85'.

'Look!' grins Chris. ' "Erected"!'

Neil says he likes it here. 'It's very relaxing; it's got none of that big-city pressure.' He poses by a long American car. 'Very *Darkness on the Edge of Town*, this is.'

We walk down to the train tracks. No one is around. We stroll into the terminal building.

'This obviously was the station,' says Chris.

'Then somebody invented the aeroplane,' says Neil.

We have walked far enough. They pose for Pennie's camera on the train tracks then Pete disappears to get the limo to pick us up.

At Kingsbury Auditorium another radio interviewer is waiting. He has an ingenious, low-budget strategy for outside broadcasts. He wants to do the interview live on air by using a portable phone which he passes back and forth. It works all right.

'What does the cover of your album mean?' he asks Chris.

'It doesn't, really,' says Chris.

In the dressing-room Sinead O'Connor's Wow! reappears. Neil drinks some with tomato juice. 'Wow!' he says. Meanwhile, outside, gay activists are handing out leaflets with pictures of the Pet Shop Boys on them.

The audience itself looks as normal as any – a little more conservatively dressed, maybe – but most of them are, we are assured, Mormons. (Everyone on the tour talks of 'Mormons' as though it were somehow akin to being an alien.) During the first song, when the dancers spell out JESUS SAVES on individual blackboards, there is usually a cheer (a mixture, I rather suspect, of those who endorse the sentiment without irony and those who appreciate its school-nightmare context). Tonight there is silence. Tonight there is a lot of silence.

At halftime Chris says, 'It's the Mrs Lowe world-view.'

Neil concurs. 'It's "They *do* have to spoil the show . . . It is a bit sick, but they're British, you know . . . The British *are* a bit sick . . ." '

During the second half I bump into Dainton, all a–fluster. He has spotted the flashes of a camera in the audience and he's looking for the culprit, but he just can't place where the flashes are coming from. He asks me to help him, and I too can see the flashes but can't spot their source. It is some minutes before we realize that they are coming from the photographer pigs, up on-stage, as they do every night.

In the dressing-room Pete photographs them both, still dressed as angels.

'I'm sorry,' declares Neil. 'I'm so good-looking on occasions. When I'm made up.'

Chris complains to Neil about his 'whoooo!' which announces the change of 'Always on My Mind' from an acoustic ballad to a high-energy romp. 'It was unconvincing and too late,' he moans. 'I'd forget that rock'n'roll stuff if I was you and stick to ironic detachment.' As he undresses Chris adds, 'Our next tour

should be called Pet Shop Boys Play The Sheds. Everything we do is so literal,' he laughs. 'Our new video is called ... "Promotion!" '

'We should call the fan club Fan Base,' suggests Neil.

People stick their heads through the door and proffer congratulations.

'I've started giving the Frank Sinatra answer,' says Neil, recalling his one encounter with Mr Sinatra. 'If people say, "It's great", I say, "Yeah, we certainly had a lot of fun on-stage tonight."' He has now decided to tackle his ailments the direct way. Champagne. 'Champagne cures everything,' he declares. 'I am an expert on the subject. I am held together by champagne on this tour.'

Some fans have been invited into the backstage catering area for a drink. I ask if any of them are Mormons. They all are. One of them tells Neil that there is to be a screening of *It Couldn't Happen Here* in town this week.

'Are you going to see it?' asks Neil. He looks at the flyer advertising the screening, and quotes from it. 'It's "unusually bizarre ... spooky ... and entertaining",' he says. 'And that's just Chris.'

Chris meanwhile is asking another group about their faith, and they are diligently relating how one of their founding fathers restored the gospel of Christ in 1830. 'If we had a book,' they say earnestly, 'we'd give it to you.'

I ask them about the rules of being a Mormon.

'No touching girls. No alcoholic drinks. No smoking. No premarital sex.' Then they tell me that the show 'was one of the best we've been to'.

But what about its religious aspects? I ask.

'I think it shows that it matters,' equivocates one.

I ask two girls whether they are encouraged to listen to pop music.

'If it's depressing, you avoid it.'

But a lot of Pet Shop Boys songs *are* depressing.

'Yeah, but not about suicide or death. If it makes you want to commit suicide.' I am about to scoff at the notion that there is any such music when she adds, rather definitively, 'I've got friends that have committed suicide because of music.'

In the limousine back to the hotel:

'We're nice people,' says Chris, meaning to have spent so much time signing autographs for the fans.

'You're not,' retorts Neil. 'You're bitter and twisted.'

Chris talks about how funny it felt pretending to be drunk in front of a crowd of Mormons during 'West End Girls'.

'You *know* we rocked them,' says Dainton. 'We burnt out the salt in Salt Lake.'

'It's now fresh water,' adds Neil, logically.

Deseret News, *Salt Lake City, 2 April, 'Pet Shop Boys put on quite a show – but what does it all mean?':*
Taking my daughter to her first rock concert was an experience neither of us will soon forget . . .

Tuesday, 2 April

In the limousine to Salt Lake City airport:

Chris had decided to stay in Salt Lake City for an extra day, but Neil travels on to Minneapolis.

'We have this ambition to do pantomime,' he says. 'We told Barbara Windsor we were going to do one with her and she was thrilled. Of course we'd be the Ugly Sisters. Kylie would be Prince Charming and Jason, of course, would be Cinderella.' He shakes his head. 'Actually it would be too camp. It would destroy our credibility for ever.'

He talks about the Salt Lake City fans from last night. 'It's amazing how in these apple-pie places you have these disconcerted kids, the rebels who don't fit in.'

At the airport he has a hot dog. 'I love these little tomato ketchup things,' he says, fingering some small sachets. 'They're very Andy Warhol.'

On the aeroplane the stewardess makes 'a special announcement for the Pet Shop Boys and their entourage, wishing them good luck on their American tour'. The entourage, who are beginning to get their own rather rowdy team spirit, cheer. The entourage now have their own rituals. When one of them shouts 'dead ants' they all must fall to the floor and imitate a dead ant.

When we land Neil decides he wants to see Prince's studios, Paisley Park, and so we drive out there. On the way he pontificates on the art of the pop film. 'I think the important thing in a pop movie is to have a plot. I've learned by experience. *A Hard Day's Night* had a plot – "Ringo's gone missing! Is the show going to happen?" – and it was fabulous myth-building for the Beatles. Like *Help!* – they all lived in one home!'

Paisley Park is not especially interesting. Prince doesn't appear. The studio manager explains lots of technical things and shows us the studios, in one of which a jazz rock group are recording. Neil says Chris would never record there anyway. 'He thought Munich was boring.' For his own part Neil doesn't want to ever record in Los Angeles. 'At least in New York, if I'm bored I can go to the theatre.'

We plan a trip to Prince's nightclub, Glam Slam.
'Do you want a car or a cab?' asks Ivan.
'Are we paying?' asks Neil.
'Yeah,' says Ivan.
'Let's get a cab,' says Neil.

Neil and I go shopping in downtown Minneapolis. He buys cassettes of the new records by REM and Joni Mitchell, this week's *New Yorker* and a copy of the academic journal *Partisan Review* because it includes an article comparing the crimes of Lenin, Stalin and Hitler.

'That's two magazines I'll never read and two tapes I'll never listen to,' he says, 'but I enjoyed buying them.'

Wednesday, 3 April

'Are you going to the show tonight?' Chris asks a fan hanging around the hotel lobby.

'Yes.'

'One of the few,' sighs Chris. 'Everyone else is going to see the Scorpions.'

He tells Neil of his day's relaxation in Salt Lake City. 'I've been converted to the Mormons. All of the Pet Shop Boys' income is going to the Mormons from now on.' He actually went tenpin bowling and up into the mountains. 'I expected it all to be little huts like Austria, but it's all concrete.' This, it seems, pleased him.

He has a question. 'Ivan, why aren't we flying to Chicago?' We are supposed to travel overnight on the bus.

'A) because it's not very far,' answers Ivan, 'and b) because we can go on the bus.'

'And c),' chips in Neil, 'because you don't *like* flying.'

'That was before I discovered Delta,' says Chris. 'They even give you a starter.'

They phone Susan Blond. They have heard that invitations have been made for their New York party and are annoyed that they haven't seen them. It is an amusing phone call to watch as it is Neil who is speaking down the phone but Chris who is, with increasing tetchiness, making most of the points, so that Neil has to relay Chris's opinions and the answers back and forth. Finally Neil tires of being the agent of Chris's anger and simply hands Chris the telephone.

'Susan?' says Chris. 'I've just been put on the phone. I don't know why.'

'I thought you wanted to say something,' mutters Neil.

'I wanted *you* to ask Susan something,' says Chris.

A few moments later, Susan Blond still on the phone, the invitation is faxed through. Chris is as livid as he expected to be. 'Basically,' he fumes, 'it's crap. It looks like an invitation to a wedding.'

'Also,' says Neil, glaring at it, 'we're not *the* Pet Shop Boys.'

They insist that it be redone.

Susan asks them to talk with *Rolling Stone*, a comment or two to accompany the photo with Axl Rose. They refuse. 'What's the angle?' huffs Neil. 'What Axl Rose said to me? We didn't really say anything.'

Once Neil has put the phone down Chris really lets rip about the invitation. 'These people have *got* to stop thinking for themselves. It's dangerous.'

'That is what these people think they are employed to do,' Neil points out.

Chris telephones Mark Farrow, their designer, in London to discuss the new party invitation. 'You weren't in bed, were you? . . . Sorry . . . Who with? . . . You're *not* on your own, are you? . . . ' The invitation sorted out, he and Neil discuss triumphantly minimal Pet Shop Boys party invitations of the past, just bearing one single phrase, with brief practical information in small type.

'I liked "Meet Liza",' says Neil. That was for a record industry meet'n'-greet with Liza.

'I thought yours was the best,' says Chris. ' "Neil Tennant – A Celebration".' Of his thirty-sixth birthday.

In the dressing-room of the Orpheum Theater the Pet Shop Boys are surprised, and not a little thrilled, to find flowers from Axl (the florist has written 'Alex') Rose. 'Congratulations on the attainment of dreams!' his note reads. 'Thanks for the hospitality. It was a beautiful night – anything but boring.'

There is, separately, a bottle of champagne with its own note. 'The bubbly goes with the flowers. Minnesota law bans champagne and flowers going together . . . '

The overture strikes up.

'I'll be glad when I never have to hear this again,' grunts Chris.

At halftime Neil confesses, likewise, 'When I'm walking off-stage at the end of "I'm Not Scared" I'm thinking, the first half's nearly over.'

'I don't suppose Prince has bothered to come,' says Chris. 'He's just a tragic rock'n'roller.'

'He's probably gone to see the Scorpions,' says Neil. 'Let's face it, he doesn't sell as many records as Axl Rose, our number-one fan.'

News arrives that the midweek British chart prediction for ' . . . Streets . . . ' is number six again.

'It's not a major hit,' moans Chris. 'I think we should ditch *Behaviour*. That turkey of an album. We should write another good dance album, write *Behaviour* off as a tax loss.' He sighs. 'We're a singles band. We're not an album band. We

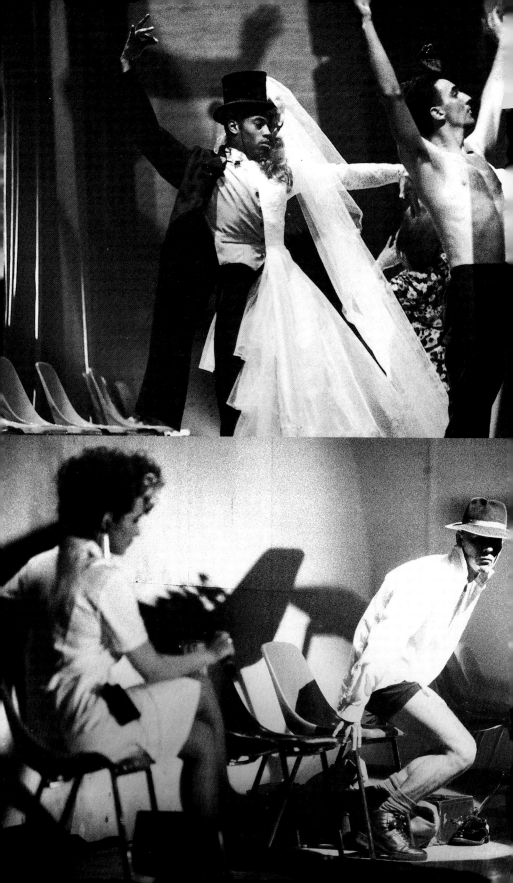

might as well not make a good album. We should make a few hit singles and then put them out with a load of rubbish.'

'Has " . . . Streets . . . " sold us any albums?' wonders Neil.

'The album's not even in the top 500,' sulks Chris quite inaccurately.

'It is in America,' protests Neil. 'It went back up to number 179.' This, alas, is precisely true.

After the show Neil browses through the *New Yorker* and comes across a cartoon where a man in pyjamas is saying goodnight and going to bed on-stage. Their joke: exactly what happens at the end of the Pet Shop Boys' performance each night. 'That's totally spooky,' Neil mutters. 'It's spooked me out.' He puts the magazine down and fusses about his stetson and his cowboy boots. Chris groans. 'Oh dear,' he says, unhappy about Neil's new-found Americana enthusiasms, 'he's on his way to being Depeche Mode.'

In an underground rectangular room beneath the venue where drinks are being taken I talk to some fans.

'The music has meaning and they showed the meaning.'

'I saw religion.'

'I saw equality for all colours.'

'People are materialist.'

'And I saw them having fun.'

'I think Chris is just the greatest. Chris is up there and he does *nothing*. He might not have a brain. He does *nothing*. It's *so* cool.'

'I liked it when he cracked a smile. Because he's having fun, but he doesn't show it.'

One of the fans excitedly tells me that he too is in a group, called Natural Selection, and they have just got a record deal. Everyone you talk to in America has just got a record deal, so I take little notice and never expect to hear the name again. Within months they have a single, 'Do Anything', near the top of the American charts.

Another fan talks to me then excuses himself. 'I gotta get out of here. I don't do basements very long.'

Someone is haranguing Neil, telling him, 'I love America, but European music is better.'

'America is obsessed by rock music,' Neil observes.

'I hate rock music,' says the fan.

'America is obsessed by rock music,' Neil repeats, 'and the sixties, in the same way that Britain is obsessed by the royal family.'

On the bus – overnight to Chicago – Neil starts playing his new cassette of REM's *Out of Time*.

'What's this?' Chris asks suspiciously.

'REM,' says Neil. 'Because I know you're a fan.'

Chicago Tribune, *4 April, 'Subtle Differences':*
'We put out complicated signals, confusing images, because we don't like the obvious thing, but I don't know if we'll ever be successful here for just those reasons,' Lowe says. 'That's why politicians talk in terms of sound bites, because you have to have one very quick idea that is instantly understandable to communicate most effectively in America. We're thinking of writing a song full of clichés and seeing how people react to that. Like "Hey, baby, I love you / everything's gonna be alright" and "We're going to find a higher ground if enough water passes under the bridge". But maybe that's too cynical – even for us.'

Thursday, 4 April

'I love Chicago,' says Neil. 'I absolutely love it. It's a *serious* city, with skyscrapers and police cars . . . They had the tallest building in the world for about three weeks, then the Toronto thing happened and that was that . . .'

He has just talked to *Rolling Stone* after all. 'It was all about Axel F,' he says. He curses, then says, worried, 'I hope I said Axl Rose and not Axel F in the interview.'

He does an interview with Fox TV. He tells them the show is 'kind of like *Cats* meets Kraftwerk'. They ask why *Behaviour* was such a mellow LP and he says, 'I hate the word "mellow" . . . more beautiful, really. I think we were quite into beauty.' Then they ask about disco and *Disco* and he launches into one of his pet theories: 'we kind of adopted the word as a kind of attitude, because we were told it was a dirty word in the States, and to us it was an undervalued type of music. For instance, the Bee Gees are highly regarded as songwriters in Britain, whereas here it was . . . white suits.'

He's on a roll now, swallowing up the topics fast as they come.

Integrity . . .

'We have a lot of integrity. I think a lot of people have very little integrity . . .' He rants about Pepsi sponsorship. 'When you come and see the Pet Shop Boys it's all content. We kind of take it seriously, but we also explore our own myth. A lot of music now is like music for commercials. Or it *is* music for commercials. It doesn't seem to be *about* anything, just references to the past . . .' He rants about specious notions that rock music is making a comeback and about how the record industry adore rock music. 'I think music should sound *now*. Pop music has to carry the burden of the past; I think it should be *about* the present.'

Diva collaborations . . .

'The only person I'd like to work with is Nina Simone. She's a fabulous singer.'

And so on. The interviewer suggests to Neil that they are like the Andrew Lloyd Webber of pop music.

'More Stephen Sondheim,' corrects Neil. 'I don't really like Andrew Lloyd Webber. Andrew Lloyd Webber is kind of like the Margaret Thatcher of pop music.'

Chris appears. It is his turn to be feeling ill (Dainton disappears to find him the inhaler), but he is enthusiastic. They are in Chicago. 'It's the best city in America – better than New York. It's New York without all the attitude.'

'I feel like this is the first *real* place,' says Neil. 'LA wasn't really real. The hotel is sort of European. I love the moment when breakfast arrives. I eat this revolting oatmeal every day. It's supposed to make you lose weight. It certainly goes right through you.'

Once again they talk about career doldrums. Neil has just spoken to a friend in England who told him that the head of a major record company was talking about how he liked every single song on *Behaviour*. It is something they have heard over and over again, far too many times. 'I think I liked it,' he says, 'when no one liked our albums, they just bought them.'

In the dressing-room they find a note from an EMI bigwig in New York suggesting a drink when they get there, and adding enthusiastically that '... Streets ... ' is a hit.

'How could he possibly know?' huffs Chris. 'It hasn't been released yet.'

It reminds Neil of the meeting they had with a man who wanted them to provide a song for the soundtrack of a film called *Pretty Woman*. 'He said, "Every woman's fantasy is to go down Rodeo Drive with someone else's credit card." '

At halftime they drink tea. There is no tap in the dressing-room and no one can be bothered to go down the corridor. 'We have tea,' Chris points out with pride, 'made with Evian water.'

The venue, the Chicago Theater, is a small, ornate, classic theatre and – as I tell them – in this setting the show is better than ever; sort of magical.

'*That's* the greatest hits title,' exclaims Chris. '*The Magic of the Pet Shop Boys*.'

'Oh, I like that,' agrees Neil.

The show is a triumph and afterwards there is a certain euphoria. 'This was *not* an easy town,' pontificates Arma. 'This was a hard town. But Chicago influences *everywhere*.'

There is a discussion about where the audiences look best.

'Very ugly tonight,' says Pete.

'They are ugly in the Midwest,' agrees Arma, 'but they're cute in Minneapolis. Corn-fed.'

A knock at the door. Tony James, previously of Sigue Sigue Sputnik and Generation X, and ex-partner of Janet Street-Porter, currently playing bass with the Sisters of Mercy, enters with their German guitarist, Andreas.

'What's it like?' Chris asks Tony, meaning touring with the Sisters of Mercy.

'Great,' he says. 'A bit like being in a dreary rock band.' He compliments them on their show. 'It must be costing a fortune.'

'We're losing a fortune,' sighs Chris.

The Sisters of Mercy are touring America in the opposite direction, East to West – going where we've been, coming from where we're going to.

'You see so many English people touring in America,' remarks Chris.

'Usually ones that you hate,' agrees Tony, 'and you're nice to them. It's so Spinal Tap.'

Chris leans towards Ivan. 'We haven't got a gig tomorrow, have we?'

'Yes,' sighs Ivan. 'We're on *tour.*'

'Is there a meet'n'glimpse now?' asks Tony.

Neil nods. 'Shall we go and talk bullshit?'

There are signatures all over the backstage walls from past inhabitants. Frank Sinatra has written 'Have a super time. I just did!' Pete writes 'Arsenal Gooners'. Dainton writes 'The Bear'.

One fan in the meet'n'glimpse is on crutches. 'I got bit by a shark,' he says apologetically. 'I was surfing.' He asks Neil for an autograph. 'Thanks a lot,' he says.

'Watch out for the sharks next time,' says Neil.

The hotel bar:

Some fans find Neil and Chris.

'Why is the *Introspective* album called *Introspective*?' asks one.

'Because we thought all the songs sounded introspective,' Neil politely replies.

A German radio interviewer has been sent over by the German promoter against the Pet Shop Boys' instructions. All day they have been refusing to have anything to do with him on principle, but finally they have been ground down. Arma leads them into a quiet room.

'It's 12.25,' Arma tells the interviewer. 'You have fifteen minutes.'

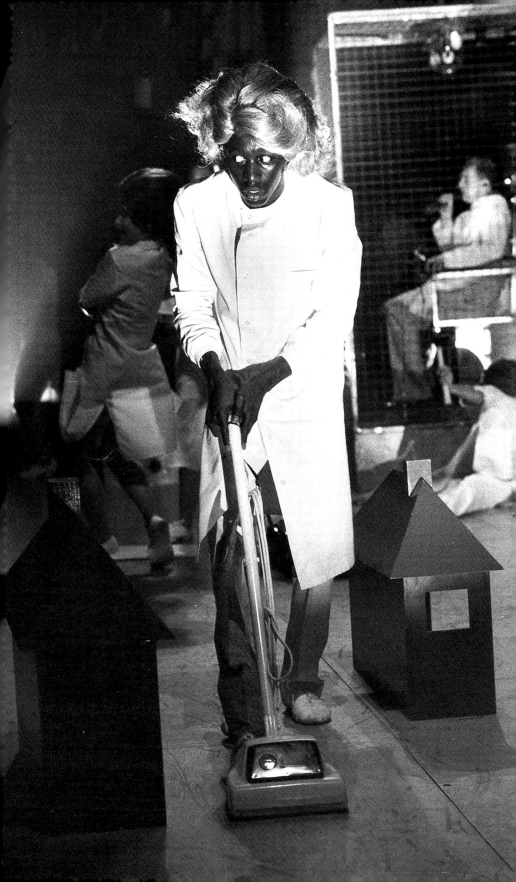

'Let's set our watches,' says Chris.

For a while Neil answers all the questions – they are all addressed to him anyway – while Chris sits there, occasionally looking at his watch and grinning at me. After about ten minutes Neil tells him to talk to Chris. He asks Chris how the songs come together.

'They're God-given,' Chris answers.

The first idea is God-given, the German suggests.

'It's not an idea,' says Chris, 'it's a talent.'

It's a craft too, the German suggests.

'It's not a craft,' scoffs Chris. 'If it was a craft *you* could do it.'

The German changes tack. Is the tour fun or distressing?

'I thought you said cross-dressing for a moment,' says Chris. 'It's fun. It's fun doing interviews at quarter to one.'

The German doesn't flinch. He asks Chris to say into the microphone 'It's gonna be all right.'

'No,' says Chris.

'Please, please,' begs the German.

'No,' grunts Chris. 'I don't perform to order.'

They head out to a nightclub called Shelter. Because they are the Pet Shop Boys, the people at the club march us into the room where people sit and simply order another set of people out of their seats so that we may sit down.

'Oh no,' says Chris, completely horrified, 'the *shame.*' When someone subsequently says, 'Pet Shop Boys? You can suck my ass', their hostility seems almost justified. One of the group Ministry comes to say hello – the club is his cousin's. We very quickly tire of sitting down anyway. It is nearly dawn when we leave.

Chicago Tribune, *5 April, 'Pet Shop Boys' other-world concert engulfs fans':*
As prostitutes, pimps, perverts, ghouls, angel-winged hit men, schoolboys in knickers, blue-suited pigs and ballet dancers fluttered around them, Tennant and Lowe remained hilariously deadpan while the audience laughed and danced. Not all the jokes worked however. 'It's a Sin' burned out on sexual overkill and the shopping-cart-world-run-amok in 'Suburbia' was more than a little obvious.

Detroit Free Press, 5 *April, 'Sound Effects – Pet Shop Boys tour in operatic grandeur':*
Most pop bands planning their first-ever tour of North America, the most lucrative music
market of all, would not hire a director and set designer whose opera productions are
regularly booed in their native Britain . . . 'In terms of opera they're pretty extreme –
they did an opera by Tchaikovsky, "Mazeppa", set in a kind of meat-packing factory,
with all the chorus dressed in white hats and overalls, chopping up meat. And the Queen
Mother was there!' . . . 'I don't want *to be booed,' Tennant, 36, says. 'It would be kind*
of interesting to be booed, but I don't know whether I have the strength of character to put
up with it, really.' . . . 'I think we have a real absence of image in America . . . We don't
live our lives in public; we've never felt very comfortable with all of that' . . . with some
amusement, Tennant notes that the duo's music was at least taken seriously by Ian
Balfour, a professor at Toronto's York University, who recently presented a respectful lecture
entitled 'Revolutions per Minute: The Pet Shop Boys Forever' on the Ivy League grounds
of Cornell University.

Metro Times, *Detroit, 3 April, 'The Perfect Dance Groove':*
Neil Tennant, the other half of the duo, says '. . . I think to an American there's
something rather creepy about us. We can't be a part of the notion "life's a party" . . .'

Friday, 5 April

In the lobby:

Neil conveys an urgent message to Chris: 'Have you talked to Jill? You've got to. There's a man who wants to paint your front door and doesn't know what colour to paint it.'

On the bus to Detroit:

Katie has been asking them to watch a video of her pop duo Puck.

'I hope it's good,' says Chris as Ivan puts it on.

It ends.

'Well . . .' says Chris and changes the subject. 'Guess what Andreas said to me last night: "Why don't you do 'Being Boring'?"'

Neil puts on a cassette of Shostakovich's Piano Concerto no. 1.

'Have you tried one of these apples?' says Pennie, brandishing three-quarters of one taken from the bus's fruit bowl. 'They're peculiar.'

'But they're a very nice colour,' Neil points out. 'With apples, that's what matters.'

We stop at a truckstop, the Wolverine Truck plaza, for a break and a snack.

'Have you read this write-up?' someone asks Neil, holding up a newspaper. 'I can't work out whether it's good or bad.'

'It's a classic "us" write-up,' sighs Neil. 'They don't like liking us.'

We reach Detroit. We aren't even stopping here for the night – after the concert we drive overnight to Washington. 'We're gypsies,' Neil tells Pete. 'This is life on the road.' We pull into the Detroit Clubland car park. Frankie Valli is playing in a theatre fifty yards down the road.

'How is your cold?' Neil asks Chris.

'It went last night.'

'It went in disco frenzy,' nods Neil, satisfied. 'I've always maintained that drinking lots of alcohol is good for colds.'

Backstage there is a fax from one of the fans from Mobile whom they had spoken to after the New Orleans show. It is a lengthy, intense letter. By the end of the first paragraph he is already saying, 'you don't just want to send whatever trivial thoughts come to mind to the person you admire and look up to in life. You have been that person for me for almost six years . . . It is important for you to understand how very seriously some of us take you, how much you mean to us.' He tells the whole story – how he had read in *Star Hits* that one of its editors (Neil) was to make a record, how he saw the 'West End Girls' video on MTV and managed to buy the single while visiting grandparents in Memphis. 'From that moment I was a Pet Shop Boys slave, a captivity I have yet to escape.' In 1988 he lost all his Pet Shop Boys memorabilia (except his records, which he was showing to a cousin) when his parents' home burnt down. He listened on. 'No one so far away had ever come so close to home.' He went to college. 'Is there success in a person who eats, sleeps and breathes and follows a band all his life?' he muses. He drove to New Orleans in his brother's car, and was in the twenty-sixth row. 'To be in the same theater with you would have been all we needed to be happy . . . my memory took permanent photographs . . . There in front of me was the man who stands in the shoes I want to wear, the man who feels the same emotions, the one so much like me only different.' In college he is studying journalism and history. Neil studied history and became a journalist. 'I want to be like you,' he writes. 'You're the friend that never goes away, the one faithfully there under every circumstance.' There are five closely typed pages, increasingly full of worship, concluding, 'If you have a little time for me, I'd love to hear from you sometime. It would make me happier than I am now, although such happiness is beyond the limits of my comprehension . . .'

Neil looks at the letter. He doesn't look happy.

I go for a walk through a shopping centre. It is shabby and run down. After a few minutes I realize that everyone I pass is staring at me. Then I realize that I am the only white person in the area. Rightly or wrongly, the message I now see in people's eyes as they pass is: you shouldn't be here. I scurry back to the venue, a little scared, and, because of that, a little ashamed.

James, the local man from EMI, is to chaperon the Pet Shop Boys to some radio stations. He talks non-stop, not just about how great the Pet Shop Boys (and Queensryche) are, but about his Piper Cherokee plane and his days as vice-president of a circus, rescuing escaped elephants in the Everglades. He says things like 'as you know, or probably know, this country has been going through a recession . . .' He tells us 'this is a very scary city. It is number two for murder.

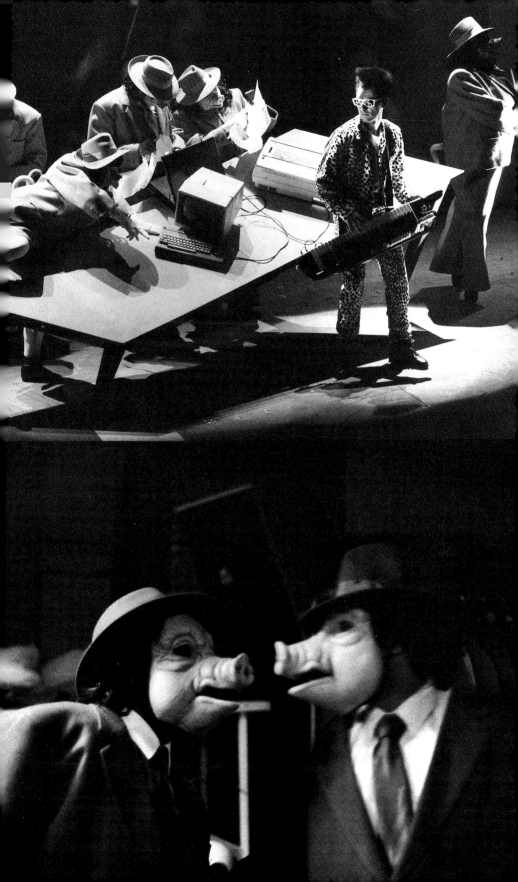

It was number one for ten years, but now that's Washington DC, where you're going...' (He sounds a little sad about this demotion of Detroit, which I suppose is understandable enough – if you're going to have that much murder you might as well top the charts.)

Whereas most of the people we meet in America take absolutely no notice of my jottings, he is intrigued by them. 'You can put in the book that my name is Hurricane,' he tells me, 'because it rhymes with Heathfield.' We arrive at a radio station where they don't seem to be expecting us at all and without much ceremony Neil and Chris are taken into a back room, asked to say some IDs and then ushered out. No interview at all.

Outside the car window Neil stares at the road sign PED XING. 'It sounds like a Chinese student leader,' he says. On the way back we drive up to the river, and get out. The other bank is Canada.

When Chris tries to get back into the concert hall from the parking lot a woman bars his way.

'I can't let you in without a pass.'

'Cancel the show!' he shouts, and turns away. Unfortunately the situation is quickly cleared up. 'I love traumas,' he says, sulking a little at the quick resolution. 'I don't like it being sorted. I like it to drag on a bit.'

Ivan tells them that the EMI man has planned a dinner afterwards. Greek.

'No plate throwing,' snaps Chris. 'We don't want to be serenaded by some guitarist waiter.'

'I think we're on to a loser here,' says Chris at halftime. 'I can feel the vibe. They're disappointed.'

Afterwards the mood is low. Everyone wants to get away, but there are important record industry people who want to shake Pet Shop Boys flesh. 'We'll have a little meet'n'greet,' Neil agrees reluctantly. 'Ten minutes. Ten people.'

'One minute each,' says Chris.

James rushes in. 'I loved it. I cried at the end.' He is followed by a man from one of America's biggest retail chains, Camelot. 'I cried all the way through. Tears down my face. We're the third-largest buyer in the United States and we're behind you.'

'Well,' says Neil, 'in that case have a glass of champagne.'

It is now that James tells them that during this Greek dinner we will be joined by 'a few friends'. They agree. 'But,' warns Chris, 'we don't want to talk about how we got our name. Or the tour.'

As it turns out, we can't even get near the Greek restaurant for a while. The coach is blocked in. Chris is livid. 'It's *such* a cock-up.'

'The only night of the tour we plan a quick getaway,' sighs Neil.

We finally reach the restaurant where James greets us and says, without a trace of irony, 'I like to go with the specials, because we're in a Greek restaurant; and when in Rome, do as the Romans do.'

There are indeed 'a few friends' here, though they appear to be the sort of 'friends' who have won a Meet the Pet Shop Boys competition. One of them immediately asks Chris, who is now in a fury, about the tour: 'Is it different every night?'

He doesn't even look up to answer. 'It's exactly the same every night.'

'Well,' sighs Neil, clambering on board the bus a while later, 'that was Detroit. It was a funny place.'

In the night, sweeping down the freeway towards Washington, we pass a convoy of coaches. Their driver talks to our driver on their CB radios and is told these are swingbeat star Keith Sweat's dancers.

'Tell him,' instructs Neil, 'our dancers are better than his dancers.'

City Paper, *Washington, 5 April:*
Their refusal to be taken-seriously pop stars combined with their pointedly unfashionable regard for Las Vegasy performahs is a paralyzing combination; no wonder their live career, until this jaunt, was limited to a 'world tour' that visited two cities, Hong Kong and London. That means this could be a once-in-a-lifetime event (assuming Tennant and Lowe don't decide they like being performahs), and even if the show is as annoying as Erasure's, the Boys' is still the most mordant music ever to call itself 'disco'.

Saturday, 6 April

A day off in Washington: in the afternoon Neil and I wander out to look at the grounds around the White House and all the museums.

We walk past a fair. 'I like merry-go-rounds,' he says. 'I've never really got over that they go up and down and around at the same time. I also like those ones with chairs that swing out. That's about as exciting as I get.'

We have a hot dog, visit the art gallery. A man, wandering past, sings 'I've got the brains – you've got the looks.'

That night about ten people dine at a smart restaurant called Domenique's. They spill sauce all over Neil's jacket and Dainton hilariously recounts having caught our coach driver masturbating in the middle of the night as he drove along.

'We'll have to change drivers,' says Pete. 'I won't be able to look at him without laughing.'

'I've always thought you'd have to be pretty kinky to be a truck driver,' says Chris. 'It's a kinky job. You sit alone all day, you pick up hitchhikers, you stop at truckstops, you sleep in your truck all day with other trucks all round.'

'You could get a contract for your summer holiday,' suggests Neil.

We discuss gossiping and Neil explains his principle of secrecy to Isabelle, one of the wardrobe people.

'Isabelle, what you've got to do is only tell one person. Then you've *hardly* told anybody, and everyone gets to know about it . . .'

Sunday, 7 April

On Sunday we convene at Washington's Bender Arena, in Room G10, the Women's Club Room – tonight the Pet Shop Boys' dressing-room. We are on the campus of the American University.

'There is no alcohol allowed,' says Neil, 'but we're going to smuggle some in.'

'Break every rule,' says Arma.

'As Tina Turner said so rightly,' says Neil.

'This is probably the most expensive private university in the country,' Arma tells us. 'Fifteen thousand dollars a year.'

'I'm not saying they have a building named after Khashoggi . . . ' says Neil, because they have. 'What university do you go to if you're rich and stupid?'

'And no good at sport,' chips in Chris.

'And ugly,' adds Neil.

'Miami,' says Arma. 'You can major in water-skiing.'

Arma has some other news. He tells them, with considerable glee, that they have the fifth best-selling import single in America.

'What are the other four?' asks Neil in rather a surly, uninterested voice.

So Arma instead talks about two of his other charges, Wilson Phillips and Cathy Dennis.

'I was thinking of putting Cathy Dennis in the group,' he says, 'and calling them Dennis Wilson.'

It is hot. Chris wants the air-conditioning put on. Apparently there are seasonal rules as to when the university air-conditioning can be put on, and early April does not qualify. The request is refused. Just before they are due to take the stage Chris announces that he will cancel the second half of the show if the air-conditioning isn't put on. The air-conditioning is switched on.

It is one of the tour's finest shows. Afterwards Neil, beaming, declares, 'Arma, this is just the start. In years to come you'll look back and say, "That was their simple tour . . . only four trucks." '

Chris, nevertheless, has found something to irk him. A Pet Shop Boys

photo done by famous Hollywood portrait photographer George Hurrell – a photo which he no longer likes – has been printed in a local newspaper.

'Arma,' he says, 'can you tell EMI to stop using this photo?'

'It was approved,' Arma points out.

'And now,' says Chris, 'it's disapproved.'

'I saw you throw your guitar pick into the audience,' Arma tells Neil.

'I *know*,' says Neil, feigning shame.

'That's so rock'n'roll,' tuts Arma, who is getting good at picking up some of the correct Pet Shop Boys attitudes.

'You *didn't*, did you?' asks Chris, horrified.

'I did,' concedes Neil, 'but I've such a pathetic throw it didn't reach the audience.'

The meet'n'greet:

A fan bounds excitedly up to Neil. He has a question.

'Have you met Whitney?'

'No,' says Neil, a little perplexed, 'we haven't.'

Katie Puckrik introduces her parents who live here. Dad – 'plays accordion and yodels' – is something important in the CIA. Katie lived in Moscow for a while when she was growing up.

'She's great,' says Neil about Katie to her father.

'She got it from her mother,' says Mr Puckrik.

Another fan begs an autograph from Neil and then says, still right in front of him, 'What a trip! I've met the dude from the Pet Shop Boys! My life's complete!'

Afterwards Neil says, 'I like America. I thought when we did this four-week trip I'd be fed up with it, but I love it. Of course, I like being liked.'

Back at the hotel, before a long evening's nightclubbing, we have a drink at the bar. Neil orders a caviar omelette. 'You know me,' he says. 'When it's all over I'm taking up Russian Studies. One of my other childhood fantasies, apart from being the Pope, was to be the Tsar of Russia.'

Someone talks about nicknames and we try to think of one for Ivan.

'I can't give Ivan a nickname,' says Neil. 'To me he's just Ivan. Ivan the Nazi.'

A woman from the hotel starts talking about her favourite Pet Shop Boys song, 'West End Boys'.

'When "West End Girls" was number one in America,' Neil reflects 'everyone was amazed, because we'd been told you couldn't succeed in America if you sounded British.' Soon he is talking about Chris's unhappiness at the loss the tour will make. 'He doesn't like it. It's like having a leak somewhere.'

'Every promoter has said "let's bring them back",' encourages Arma. 'This is the biggest thing that's happened in America in rock'n'roll.'

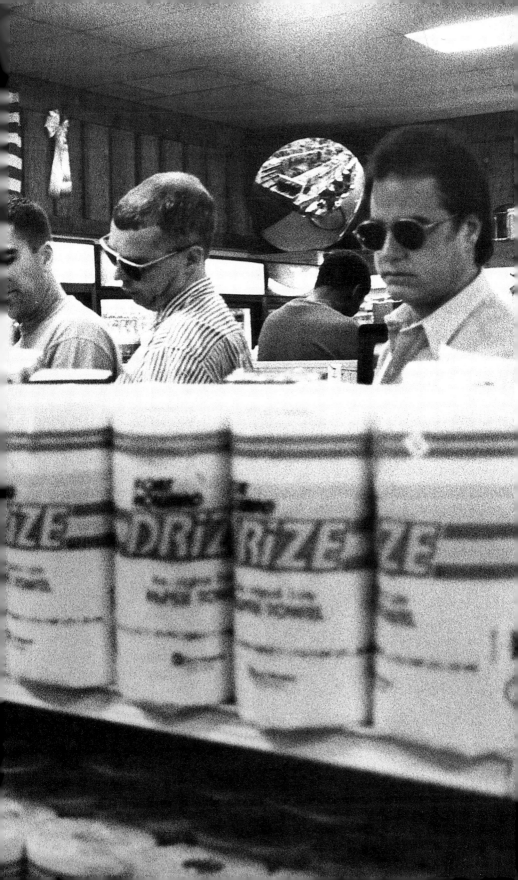

Monday, 8 April

Arma's plan has always been that, once this month-long tour has proved itself a success, the Pet Shop Boys would return in the summer to play the sheds. On the bus journey to New York he runs through the finances. Right now the show costs $220,000 every week to keep on the road. Assuming that would rise to $250,000 when they returned, if they can get five shows a week with guarantees from promoters of $50,000 — and he says they can — then the percentage earnings on top of that when concerts are well attended, and the money from merchandising, would all be profit. Neil and Chris listen but they don't say much. 'All those truckers,' says Chris, glancing out the window, 'look like mass murderers.'

Ivan takes them through various items of New York business. They approve (and, in certain cases, disapprove) the party guest list. He warns them that at Radio City Music Hall they must do everything on time — 'it's a union mafia thing' — and tells them that the EMI executives want a photo taken with the two of them.

'No,' says Neil.

'No,' says Chris.

One of the guest list names (approved) is Shep Pettibone, a man who remixed several of their singles when he was a barely known underground dance music engineer, but who recently co-wrote and produced 'Vogue' with Madonna. 'He's obsessed with the idea that we should do another "West End Girls",' says Neil.

'So is everyone,' grumbles Chris.

'I've got an idea for a "West End Girls" type song,' says Neil. 'It's called "DJ Culture".'

Chris turns to Pennie. 'Pennie,' he complains, 'is smoking on our *no-smoking coach*. The one thing I can't stand is the smell of smoking with fruit on coaches.'

The bus draws up near, but not in front of, the Royalton Hotel. 'I don't know what we're doing,' says Chris, 'letting these two-bob dancers stay in a hotel like this.'

Trevor stands in the lobby, perplexed. 'A very bizarre person designed this,' he says.

'He's on a learning process, isn't he?' says Chris, rather sweetly. 'The amount of accumulation going on, it's like sending a satellite into space. He's such a star.' Pause. 'He can't sing, though, can he?'

'He wants to have singing lessons,' says Neil. 'He's already talked to me about it.'

Neil is given a thick wad of paper which has been faxed to Yon at Susan Blond's office. It is the lecture by the Toronto academic Ian Balfour called 'Revolutions per Minute or The Pet Shop Boys Forever'. He sends with it a covering note. 'I hope you won't find my piece on your work too academic or funereal – perhaps I should apologize for taking you too seriously. It may well come across as pretentious in some places – part of that is a deliberate strategy to level the differences between the ways people talk about high and pop culture respectively.'

It begins 'the ideal Pet Shop Boys song lasts forever', a notion which he chooses to illustrate with extensive quotation from, and discussion of, 'It's Alright'. He goes on to discuss their 'pervasive preoccupation with infinity'; this 'infinitizing' he sees as characteristic of several strands of pop music since the sixties. He draws out ideas of structural infinity and syntactical open-endedness so that he can soon refer to 'Love Comes Quickly' as a song where 'the grammar of infinity is thematized in erotic terms'. Amid the heady intellectualism there are some quite awful puns (sometimes the posited structural similarity that allows the pun is the point, sometimes not) so that when he discusses the line 'Che Guevara and Debussy to a disco beat' it is no surprise that he comments that their 'vision of the revolution comes with strings attached'. His argument spirals around to the 'Being Boring' video, a video of a song which, he says, is their only song 'where one is confronted with thinking of an end'. And here he welds his themes with his final sentence: 'For the music goes on and on forever – it has to go on and on – because in the logic of the Pet Shop Boys, silence equals death.'

We visit the party building for an inspection.

'It's just no good,' says Chris immediately. He demands a smoke machine and flower strobes. 'I might not even come,' he says.

Kiki Mason arrives, spraying kisses, and takes them through the plans. Susan Blond checks through her guest list of invited celebrities. At one name they sneer.

'I thought he was famous,' Susan apologizes.

A few names later they pour scorn on a group.

'You don't like them either?'

'We don't like anyone,' says Chris, 'so carry on.'

Kiki says there will be a video screen – 'no Pet Shop Boys,' he sensibly assures them. 'I think none of it should make sense.'

They nod approvingly.

'Do lasers cost a lot of money?' asks Chris.

'Lasers are hard to install,' demurs Kiki.

'Because,' explains Chris, 'I can just stand in lasers for hours and I'm very happy. There's one at Blackpool and I just stand in the middle for ages.' This discussion has cheered him up. 'Well,' he says, 'I'm sorry, I'm looking forward to the party.'

'I get nervous thinking about it,' says Neil. 'All those people.'

'You just get off your nut,' advises Chris.

Kiki tells them Madonna might come. Lady Miss Kier has sent a postcard apologizing. 'I couldn't get Ivana Trump,' Kiki confesses. 'I'm sorry. She said, "I'm doing this thing at the Plaza and it's the first thing I've done with the Donald since the divorce. It's going to be a zoo!"'

'Why is she doing it?' asks Chris.

'Because they really push the Plaza,' Kiki explains. 'She's such a good businesswoman. She shakes everybody's hand and gets their life story. She must have read one of those books that say, "hold someone's hand firmly and look into his eyes as if you care about them . . . "'

New Yorker, *8 April, 'Jazz/pop/rock personal appearances':*
There is no band, and almost everything is on tape, computer-generated. But there will be lots of backup singers, beautiful dancing boys, more costume changes than at a Cher concert, and, at the center of it all, the man who has raised ennui to a Pop Art form, Neil Tennant. He and his button-pushing partner, Chris Lowe, construct electronic washes with catchy choruses . . . Post-modern madness, and never boring, this could be the silliest extravaganza New York has seen since the glory days of the Tubes.

Tuesday, 9 April

Ivan has warned everyone not even to speak to any of the staff at Radio City Music Hall. One wrong move and they'll cancel the show. Neil is accosted by one and, obeying orders, he doesn't react, but once he's behind closed doors he fumes. 'They're all Nazis,' he says. 'There aren't any left-wing unions in America – they're all bunches of Nazis. "Who is you?" he says. I'm the *singer* ...' He sighs. 'You have to relax. I feel like taking on the whole thing single-handed.'

Neil is puzzled by the fact that Liza Minnelli hasn't been in touch. 'I think she thinks we're going to ask her to appear on-stage and she doesn't want to do it.' As it happens this has been considered. They have been thinking it might be wonderful if, for 'Rent', a figure stepped from the wings and, this time, it was not Sylvia but Liza.

'Did we ask her?' asks Chris.

'No, we didn't,' answers Neil.

Arma sweeps in. 'We have,' he announces, 'got a big display in Sam Goody's.' Sam Goody's is a big record shop just down the street.

'Who organized that?' asks Neil. 'Surely not EMI?'

'I think they must have,' says Arma. 'I can't take credit for that.'

'Arma,' scolds Neil, 'we should take credit for *everything.*'

One of the ongoing technical problems has been the failure to find a workable type of snow to pour down on top of Neil and Chris during 'My October Symphony'. (In rehearsals they used soap flakes that made the sloped area of the stage too slippery to walk on.) At today's soundcheck they learn that, for New York at least, there is snow: plastic snow. Neil shows it to the dancers – 'like dandruff,' he explains – then starts singing Kool and the Gang's 'Get Down On It'. He tells Trevor that there is a piano in his dressing-room 'so you can have the first singing lesson'.

'Is Madonna coming?' Trevor asks Neil.

'Sadly not,' says Neil, 'though there is a *rumour* that she is coming. Probably started by us.'

Neil leads Trevor upstairs. 'What you've got to do is sit down on this stool, sit up like this so your back is straight, then take a really big breath until you can feel it in your back. You've got to be relaxed. Don't be tense ... you shouldn't let your shoulders go up. Sing from down here, not up there. Go "Aaaaaaaaaaahhhhhhhhhh" ...'

Trevor laughs, and doesn't do it, but after Neil cajoles him some more he does, at first very weakly and feebly.

'Your muscles here' – Neil points to his face – 'should be relaxed. I always get told off by my singing teacher.' Now Neil begins taking him up the scale. 'Do CDE ...'

'This isn't going to get out,' worries Trevor, 'that I was doing this, right?'

On the lesson goes. Neil seems a good teacher, by turns encouraging and unforgiving. He stretches Trevor at both ends of his voice until Trevor mutters, 'They might call the cops soon.'

Chris walks in. 'I need a couch. I want to lie down.'

'We're having singing lessons in here,' says Neil.

Trevor's wish for secrecy is a little disingenuous. When the whole cast is crowded together eating dinner he says loudly to Neil, 'You didn't tell anybody, did you?'

'No,' replies Neil, at equal volume, 'I didn't tell anyone I've been giving you singing lessons.'

'We've made it,' sighs Neil, sinking into the dressing-room sofa. 'We've sold out at Radio City Music Hall. We'll go bankrupt now.'

'It'll all be over, just like that,' echoes David Alden, trying to get into the spirit.

'I quite like the slow slide,' says Neil. 'The worst ones are the desperate ones like Oscar Wilde: you go to prison for buggery, lose all your money and your children change their names ... few people have been so ruined as Oscar Wilde. They had a public auction on Tite Street of all these signed first editions, and when he went on trial he had three plays on in the West End and you couldn't mention his name. Consequently, he became a legend, but it's hard to shock people that badly.'

David Alden ponders. 'I'm not sure what you could do.'

Neil smiles. 'I'm sure Chris will come up with something.'

The conversation drifts on and Neil begins to pontificate a little: 'The problem about America is you get all these women, all these fabulous women like Barbra Streisand and Liza Minnelli and Diana Ross and then they do terrible films and bad records and ruin their careers. Of course the problem is, they should be allowed to have no control. They should exist in a Hollywood star system. Make four films a year: one would be good, one great and two shit . . . Barbra Streisand, one of the greatest Broadway stars ever, doesn't go *near* Broadway. That's the trouble . . . and every choreographer has died of AIDS. And who do you get to write the songs? It's a dinosaur breed . . . This, of course, is what I think will happen to Madonna. She'll suddenly be like a beached whale. She won't be good enough and she'll want control. Maybe she'll just learn to act . . . She was good in *Dick Tracy*, but she needs to play glamour or to play a prostitute, and there's a limit to how many you can do . . . The president of Touchstone came to the show in LA. I thought, wow! We're going to get a three-picture deal at 10.30. We never heard anything . . . '

'I can imagine this being a very funny audience,' worries Chris. 'I'm anticipating the worst reaction. It'll be a real kind of "impress us" crowd.'

Someone comes in with a new keyboard for Chris – there is a problem with the usual one. He is utterly freaked out. 'Oh no! I can't cope with that at the last minute! I don't like things being changed at the last minute.' He tries it on. 'Can you make the strap a bit longer? I want it real punky. Like Hooky.'

Two pieces of money information arrive simultaneously: Arma's thrilled announcement that tickets are being scalped outside for between $50 and $75, and Robbie's rather more sobering revelation that if they overrun tonight it will cost them $1,800 to buy union time up until 11.00 p.m.

Liza Minnelli does turn up after all, swooping into Neil's dressing-room and telling Neil about the British première of her forthcoming film *Steppin' Out*.

'Will you take me?' she asks.

'Of course,' he says.

Liza has a forthcoming residency here. The two of them swap tales about who is going to lose the most money. She tells Neil, 'I said I wanted it to look like the Pet Shop Boys and everyone looked at me.' She describes how it does actually look: 'There's a giant shoe . . . '

'A giant shoe?' Neil echoes. 'That's great.'

They talk about current musicals.

'Did you see *Miss Saigon*?' Neil asks. 'Everyone says the helicopter is good.'

'I took Michael Jackson to *Les Miserables*,' she answers. 'It went down and I thought, is that *it*? We're sitting here with all that security for *that*?'

Liza wants Neil to see some of her show. 'I could do a run-through for you,' she offers.

'It would have to be tomorrow, before three o'clock,' he says.

'OK,' she says.

'What if I come over about midday?' he says. 'Are you doing any songs from the album?'

'I'm doing "Losing My Mind",' she says.

'I think you should do "Rent",' he says.

'I tried to,' she apologizes, 'but it's the *pacing*...'

It turns out that she can't wait to share her show. 'I want to show you my opening,' she says and, here and now, she begins to act it out, and to sing the first song. Then she says, 'I've got to go and see Chris.'

'I think he's asleep,' Neil tells her.

She pops her head into his dressing-room then returns. 'He *is* asleep,' she says, though quite quickly he wakes up and appears.

'I hear you and Shep and Madonna went nightclubbing,' he says.

'It wasn't nightclubbing,' she demurs. 'We went to this serious drag club with Steven Meisel. You would have walked out when I did.'

'What's Madonna like?' asks Neil.

'She's great,' answers Liza. 'She comes from Queens and she doesn't pretend she doesn't.'

'Where's your dog?' Chris asks.

'Lilly? I can't bring Lilly into Radio City,' she says. She holds out her arms to emphasize her body. 'Look at me! I'm so thin!'

'You're always thin,' says Chris.

'It's from tap-dancing,' she says. She picks at the food on the table. 'I'm stealing your M&Ms. What's the party going to be like?'

'Great,' says Chris.

'Are we finally going to have a rave-up?' she asks.

'Yup,' replies Chris.

'All right,' she says. 'I'm ready.' She lights up a Marlboro.

'I think it's a shame you're not doing "Rent",' says Neil.

'I might still do it,' she says. 'Can I smoke or will it drive you mad?'

'It's OK,' says Neil. He sighs contentedly. 'We're having such a life. This tour is such a circus.'

'I'm so glad you're losing money,' she smiles. 'I thought I was the only one.'

'We're losing it hand over fist,' says Neil, 'and Chris is *mean!*'

She sighs. 'I'm so pleased to see you. I love you and I miss you.'

Alan pops his head in the door. 'I've come to nag you – ten to fifteen minutes.'

She picks up Neil's lipstick and tries it on, then takes her leave. 'Bye! Oh, this is *so* exciting!'

Meanwhile, with five minutes left, Chris and Alan argue about socks. Chris says the two he's been given are not a pair; Alan insists they are.

'Let's do the dangly test,' says Chris, and triumphantly dangles them so that their different lengths hang side by side. Alan finds some more.

The dressing-room is high above the stage. Neil refuses to take the lift and instead walks down the stairs. 'I'm scared it will get stuck.'

Chris takes the lift. 'I'm hoping it does.'

Halftime:

'They're a dreary audience,' sighs Chris. 'As predicted.'

'It's not a disaster,' says Neil.

'A lot of people might not be coming back after the fifteen minutes,' retorts Chris.

'I did see someone walk out in the fourth number,' says Neil.

'And that was Liza,' sniggers Chris.

David Alden comes in.

'Well,' sighs Chris, 'it's a difficult crowd.'

' "Sophisticated" is the word,' says David Alden.

' "Wry",' says Chris.

They go to separate dressing-rooms. When Chris's wig arrives he says, 'Neil's in his own room – *twice* the size of mine.' This time this is, as it happens, true.

Arma appears. 'New York is a tough audience,' he says. 'They're tough on *anyone*. They're tough on *Elton John*.'

'So,' says Neil, faking indifference, 'OK, New York doesn't like us. Someone has not to like us.'

Ivan appears.

'It's a tough crowd, Ivan,' says Neil. 'They've seen it all before.'

'I hate stuffy audiences,' Ivan huffs. 'If they don't stand up in "Always on My Mind" they can all fuck off.'

Neil sighs. 'Still, they've got the good half now. It's not over till it's over.'

And back they go, Neil by the stairs, Chris by lift.

Afterwards:

'*What* a dreary crowd,' says Pete.

'Just so you know, this is not untypical for New York,' insists Arma.

'They were watching it more,' considers Neil. 'It took off in "Opportunities" as usual.' He sighs. 'I bet we get shit reviews. I bet *Rolling Stone*, the whole gang, slag it off.'

'Who gives a shit?' says Ivan. 'Who gives a fuck?' He pauses a moment. 'Well, actually we all do. We care quite a lot...'

Liza glides in and heads towards Neil: 'Hi, baby, it was fantastic!'

'What a tough crowd,' says Neil.

'They were *startled*,' interprets Liza. 'It was stunning. Did you hear me scream at you?'

'I have these headphones,' he apologizes, shaking his head. 'Sometimes it's like I'm not there.'

'Did you see the mad guy at the front?' she asks.

'He was a real serial killer,' nods Neil. 'I pointed at him, during one of the pointy bits.'

'Hi, baby,' Liza coos at Chris. 'Nice dancing.' She tries to imitate his steps.

'You've got to do it in your underwear. The Calvin Klein.'

'The ones I gave you?' she asks.

'No,' he explains, 'it's the new ones we're all wearing. They're between underpants and boxer shorts.'

Sal Licata enters.

'Sal, hi!' says Neil.

Outside the stage door are a gaggle of fans.

'I touched him!' one shouts.

'Awesome, Chris!' shouts another.

'Chris, do you really shave your legs?' asks a third.

'No,' he says.

'Do you know Frank Sidebottom?' inquires a fourth.

'Do I?' wonders Chris, momentarily taken aback. 'I don't think so.'

They each pile into a limousine.

'We're in separate cars,' hoots Neil. 'It's so decadent. It's like we don't speak.'

Neil is a little perplexed by the whole Radio City Music Hall experience, especially the entourage who came backstage with Liza. The photographer Steven Meisel just stood there, without saying a single word. 'I think it's a bit rude to come backstage and not say anything. It's a real trendy way of behaving.' He's also a little paranoid about Liza's true opinion of what she saw. 'Liza judges everything with very very *professional* criteria. I kind of felt that she wasn't really knocked out by it. It's sort of a pity, because I thought it might do well here, and it's sort of been a bit disappointing. I felt very unprofessional on that stage. I guess that's what concerns me, that I wasn't good enough to be there . . . '

On the way to the party:

'Eartha Kitt watched the whole performance in sunglasses,' laughs Neil, who seems both offended and rather impressed by this.

Chris predicts that they won't get into their own party.

'You will,' Ivan insists.

'We couldn't take on New York,' sighs Neil. 'Pet Shop Boys versus America – we lost in the end. We were doing so well . . . '

'The party will be crap,' predicts Chris.

'We can enjoy it or not,' counsels Neil. 'We're not about this kind of thing.'

'It's so shameless, arriving in a limo,' says Chris.

'It's what we all do,' says Neil.

We pull up outside. It's around 12.30. The paparazzi ask them to pose.

'Can we do a few shots?' Neil asks Chris.

'No,' he says. Neil looks at him. 'I'm not going to stop them,' Chris says.

'So you're saying yes,' says Neil.

We go in. (No metal detector, of course.) Upstairs – in the VIP area – it is more crushed than downstairs. Michael Musto, a columnist from *Village Voice*, asks them for comments. Jean Paul Gaultier tells them, beaming, 'It's a real real real show . . . each song was strung on a real story. When you were angels in the bed, it was beautiful.' Bruce Weber hands round gentle compliments. Then Neil is imperiously summoned to meet Eartha Kitt, sitting in a corner.

'It was a little noisy for me,' she tells him, 'but I found it fascinating. I'd like to come and see it when it's less noisy.'

Neil nods politely. 'I saw you in *Follies* three times,' he tells her. 'It was such a great production, that.'

Susan Blond keeps encouraging them to have their photo taken. It is a very New York idea – you spend all your time at your own party having your photo taken and talk to newspaper columnists so that you are *seen* to have had a great party. A journalist approaches Neil.

'Are you . . . ?' he asks.

'I'm one of Depeche Mode,' he tells him.

It is packed tight, and very hot.

'My shirt is literally soaked,' says Neil. 'I could have been under a shower. This suit will probably have to be destroyed.'

He decides to leave. Chris stays, dancing through most of the night. A small posse catches a cab to an all-night restaurant Lox around the Clock. 'I've changed my mind,' says Neil. 'I've decided it's a triumph.'

Patrick, a writer friend of Neil, says he was sitting next to Liza. 'She was singing the ones she knows,' he says. 'She was getting really excited.'

'I thought Eartha Kitt would be completely *gone*,' says Neil, 'but she was completely there. She gave me her address and said, "Liza says you write such interesting lyrics."'

Neil orders soup.

'All they wanted to do in the club was to take drugs and have sex,' tuts another friend, Jon Savage, 'and all Neil wants to do is eat vegetable soup.'

'Liza,' mutters Neil, 'asked me a surprising question: how many trucks do you have? I wouldn't have thought she'd be involved in that.'

'Did you notice,' says Jon Savage, 'that on the back of the backstage passes it said, "Say no to drugs"?'

'That's terrible,' says Neil. He is finding a second wind. 'I suppose it's too late,' he says, 'to go back to the party . . . '

The New York Times, *11 April, 'Serious Spectacle From the Pet Shop Boys':*
Madonna, David Bowie, Alice Cooper and Pink Floyd now have serious competition . . . Most of the Pet Shop Boys' songs are unassertive ditties set to unabashedly mechanical electro-pop, perking along with a light boom-chicka-boom . . . Mr Tennant maintained an unfailing art-popster's deadpan on stage . . . From repressed schoolboys to masochistic lovers, from artists stranded by world events to pop stars sequestered by fame, the narrators of Pet Shop Boys songs don't share much human contact, much less kindness . . . the

plaintive-sounding Mr Tennant and the silent Mr Lowe . . . the performance showed that
the Pet Shop Boys know all about artifice, yet they haven't forgotten that pop's formulas
can crystallize genuine emotions.

New York Daily News, *11 April, 'Pet Shop Boys: Mind Over Motion':*
. . . enough gruesome props, freakish costumes and corrosive personas to suggest a version
of 'Satyricon' as enacted by the entire Met Opera on Ecstasy . . . If you had to pick one
word for this show — besides brilliant — it would be busy . . . since the stars are, by their
own admission, about as charismatic as your tax accountant, it was practically a prerequisite
to stress theatrics over musicianship . . . with so much visual information thrown at the
audience — and in such an arch and chilly manner — it was impossible to respond viscerally.
So why did it work so well? Well, the Pet Shop Boys' appeal has always been in making
a compulsively uptight point of view thrillingly poignant . . . True, the show's distancing
grandness may have only stressed their self-involvement, but it upped their radicalism . . .
if the Pet Shop Boys didn't make us move our feet, they made our minds dance, sweeping
us away with a refined kind of nerve.

New York Newsday, *11 April, 'Gaudy Creatures in the Pet Shop':*
The Pet Shop Boys' show at Radio City Music Hall Tuesday night had the horrible
fascination of a 26-car turnpike pileup . . . That such tremendous money and care clearly
went into this show seems a throwback to the Excessive Eighties. It's no surprise that one
of the group's hits is called 'Opportunities (Let's Make Lots of Money)'. Tennant and
Lowe don't have much talent, but they imitate it well. The Pet Shop Boys are the musical
equivalent of junk bonds . . . 'It's a Sin' is a blatant rewrite of Barry Manilow's 'Could
It be Magic?' . . . The show begs for someone who can bring a sense of fun to the Pet
Shop Boys' arid camp excesses . . . It aspires to grand kitsch; it is a grand bore.

New York Post, *11 April, 'Call 'em Pet Slop Boys':*
In a stunning display of pretentiousness — so overdone, underthought and outrageous that
it was hardly recognizable as a pop-music performance — the Pet Shop Boys made their
New York debut . . . Tuesday's outing feebly attempted to bring life to the duo's songs . . .
Call me picky, but I want to see who's making the music . . . the revolting opening
English schoolboy number, which ended with simulated masturbation; a couple of racially
obscene skits, with a black man being led around the stage on a chain leash attached to

his spiked dog collar . . . After a show like this, Radio City Music Hall should install windows to air the place out . . . Tennant was strapped into an electric chair for a mock execution while fifth-wheel Lowe played a dog-boy caged on the opposite side of the stage. Too bad concert director David Alden wasn't strapped into ol' sparky for a jolt or two himself . . . The sad thing is the Pet Shop Boys are really serious about their 'art'.

Wednesday, 10 April

I walk with Neil up to Radio City Music Hall in the morning to watch Liza rehearse. She and her dancers are just about to stop when we arrive, but she makes them stay and insists that they act out the whole final number – the tap-dance finale 'Steppin' Out' – just for our benefit. It is an amazing scene: Liza Minnelli dancing, singing and tap-dancing this show-stopper for an audience of two, sometimes just a yard in front of us.

She reflects about the merits of their show. 'It was performance art. It all made no sense. People here are always looking for a *theme*.'

Neil nods. 'It's not really possible to take a load of songs that weren't connected before and to string them together into a story so that you go, "Oh, the butler did it... "'

Liza also politely mutters that Katie should wear a G-string. 'You can,' she says, 'see her pubes, and no one wants to see them.'

Backstage. Neil is on the phone to an American journalist friend David Keeps.

'*Rolling Stone* were nice. They've finally got over the fact that John Lennon died, though they still haven't realized that the Rolling Stones are crap ... That Doors film: a) is it crap? or b) is it crap? You just think Jim Morrison is a wanker and a third-rate talent. I went to see it my first day in America to get in a bad mood about everything ...'

'We're shifting gears,' Arma announces. 'I have thirty major promoters flying in and I have a dinner with them afterwards.' He talks through the potential earnings if they return – now it's 'a hundred thousand dollars a night in tickets and forty to fifty thousand dollars in merchandise'. The promoters are keen. 'There's no Depeche Mode out there, no Erasure, so they think they can do the business ... I don't want to categorize your fans, but these people have to go somewhere ...'

'I'm quite happy for you to categorize our fans,' says Neil.

Chris is a little piqued by something Ivan told him, and something he has subsequently discovered.

'Ivan *did* go out last night,' he says. 'I don't like it when people lie. I'm going to have a word with him about it . . . '

'He doesn't have to tell us everything he does,' Neil objects. 'That's what you call a white lie.'

'Well, I don't like white lies,' grumps Chris.

Arma phones up Jack Satter, who enthuses about last night's show.

'Did Jack Satter come last night?' mutters Chris suspiciously. 'I didn't see him there. I don't believe he went.'

'Jack,' says Arma, down the phone, 'Chris would like to thank you for showing up last night.'

Lynne relates something Trevor has said to her: 'This hotel is weird. It's a Chris Lowe hotel, full of satanic horns everywhere . . . '

We take out a few of the cast, including Trevor and Mark dressed as angels, to do some photos on the New York streets. Trevor, in particular, is feigning unhappiness while loving the attention, hamming it up while claiming it to be one of the most embarrassing moments of his life.

'In New York,' Neil points out, 'no one is even going to look at you, dressed as an angel.'

By and large this turns out to be true.

Back at Radio City they look at some photos of themselves.

'I don't think we do smiling very well,' says Chris. 'We just look very smarmy and self-centred, as if we think we're marvellous. Anyway, smiling wasn't forced in the beginning, but it is now. I can't be bothered with it now.'

Dainton announces that the tale of the *Tonight Show* walk-off is in the *Mirror* and the *Sun*. 'The *Sun* says,' he relates, 'Pet Shop Brat.'

'I must get some "spoilt brat" T-shirts made up,' says Chris.

Arma comes in. 'I have three promoters – '

'I don't want to meet them,' Chris interrupts.

'I'll announce you, say, "This is Chris Lowe," ' suggests Arma, 'and you don't even have to speak. You don't have to make eye contact.'

'OK,' he consents.

'They don't even want to meet you anyway,' taunts Pete. 'They want to meet Neil. They think you're one of the dancers; a sidekick.'

'That's another T-shirt I should have made: "Sidekick".'

'Much better than last night,' sighs Neil after tonight's show. 'The crowd was moderately cheerful.'

Chris shares his 'spoilt brat' idea.

'Spoilt Brat!' exclaims Neil, thrilled. 'It's a good title for a song. I'm going to write it down. What you should do is be shameless and make a T-shirt and then send a photo to the *Sun*: "I'm unrepentant," says Chris Lowe . . .'

Arma pops in. 'The promoters have gone to the restaurant, so you don't have to do it.'

'Good,' says Chris, 'it'd only spoil it if they meet us.'

'Get the money first,' agrees Neil, 'before we meet them and say something wrong.' He thinks. 'They like it?'

'Yes,' says Brad, their booking agent.

'Up the money!' he exclaims, like a battle cry.

Some semi-celebrities trickle backstage: Nona Hendryx, Mick Murphy from the System. ('Ah, the System!' says Neil.) Nona is, it turns out, also a friend of Dusty Springfield.

'We all know Dusty,' Neil explains to Arma. 'It's like a club.'

Trevor sits in the foyer of the Royalton in a daze. As he often does he just begins to talk, and then free-associates on and on and on: 'This hotel is like a bad dream. I had a dream like this once. Like "It's a Sin"', there's horror everywhere. I don't want subtle sexual metaphors, I want a good night's sleep. It's like waking up with an ugly girl with bad breath looking at you. This hotel just freaks me out. There's a fireplace with no fire, but a chequered flag in it. What do you want a chequered flag for? You want a fire to keep you warm. It's like something out of *Nightmare on Elm Street 5*. Look at the lights! They're dark! You want a light so you can see, not so that it's pretty. This couch has no back; it's no good for my back, it's no good for my neck, it's no good for me. Can I get a witness? – this hotel is freaked out. They've got these big pillars and you don't *need* them. You could walk into these pillars, it's so dark. There's white linen hospital bed sheets on the chair. It's insulting, like your butt's too dirty to sit down. I feel institutionalized. It's like a mental hospital. These lifts are like being in a shower. Have you ever heard of claustrophobia? These people have so much attitude. The people who work here look like out of a kung fu film. I've walked past the cashier about a hundred million times. It's like one of those public toilets you pay to get in. The whole room is so sharp. It's full of right angles. Nothing is curved. Nothing is classic. Look at the fish – they look bored. Bored out of their minds. There's only one fish in each, not a mummy fish and daddy fish. That's persecution. They put fish in different bowls so they can look at each other and not get it on. It's like window-shopping without any money. A male fish is saying, "You look fine, but I can't jump over to you", so they curl up and die. Fish need love too. Just like divas. The corridor is like a maze. Like Hampton Court but worse. It's like mice and cheese. It's like the Bible: Revelations 12, verse 9. The place looks like a bank. Why is it fifteen dollars for one cheeseburger with chips that weren't even chips? It's the horns. The whole place is just freaked out. You can't relax. It's an Alfred Hitchcock hotel. Why have the horns got lights on them? *Please*. Look at the plants. They look decrepit and forlorn . . . '

Village Voice, *New York, 15 April, 'Where The Boys Are':*
. . . the closest pop has come to surrealist stagecraft since Jean-Paul Goude concocted Grace Jones's radically theatrical One Man Shows . . . Both Boys affect the glazed deadpan of runway models; no matter what happens (they're stuck in those cages, pawed over, kicked about, taunted, and electroshocked), they're blasé as shit . . . It was all brilliantly over-the-top, flamboyantly theatrical, and casually, matter-of-factly gay . . . By way of declaring the trad rock show dead, the Pet Shop Boys have found a way to bring it back to extravagant life.

Village Voice, *New York, 15 April, 'La Dolce Musto':*
By the 50th mock blowjob, a procession of pigs with valises did a conga . . . At their Building party . . . blasé Pet Shop Boy Neil Tennant murmured, 'They promised us an area where we could hang out with 10 people,' as he was swarmed by glittering sociopaths.

Thursday, 11 April

On the train to Boston they survey Mark Farrow's artwork roughs for the sleeve of their new video compilation, *Promotion*. They don't like them.

'He's really boobed this time,' says Chris. 'He's tried to make us look like the Farm. I don't know what the hell he's playing at.'

'All he has to do is change the typography,' says Neil.

'But that was all he had to do in the first place,' complains Chris. 'Even the one that's OK is crap.'

Neil takes out his *Portable Dorothy Parker* and the conversation is left behind. The artwork roughs are tucked into the luggage rack where, accidentally, they too will be left behind.

'I don't know why we didn't fly,' Chris says after about an hour of rolling suburbia.

'We don't fly,' Neil reminds him, 'because you don't like it.'

They discuss the possibility of the tour returning here.

'I think there's all these people who've been waiting to see us since "West End Girls" and now they'll just tick us off their list,' says Chris.

'Arma, of course, knows in his heart of hearts he'll never get us back after this,' says Neil.

Ivan sits across the way, asleep, and we can hear *Introspective* leaking from his headphones.

'Our music just goes on and on, doesn't it?' says Chris. He listens some more. 'The vocals are very loud, aren't they?'

'The deadpan vocals?' says Neil. 'The ironic detachment? The plaintive vocabulary? What amuses me about the reviews is that they think we could do something else if we wanted to, that we've made a deliberate decision...'

'I don't think that after this tour we should play any of our old songs ever again,' says Chris.

'Maybe a farewell tour,' says Neil.

'This is it,' says Chris. He tells us about his 'really good dream' last night. 'I was in *Dr Who* and the drawings on the carpets were satanic messages. It had chases and everything.'

'So,' sighs Neil, 'Madonna's snubbed us. Though,' he says, perking up, 'she might come to Paris.'

Who said that? I ask.

'I just made it up,' he says. He looks at the countryside. 'I'd like a five-day break in the country, swimming, a roaring fire for those chilly evenings, intelligent conversation, a little light jogging, a fine French chef and the occasional murder for Angela Lansbury to solve . . . '

They swap party chat.

'Bruce Weber,' says Neil, 'thought the show was "gorgeous".'

'That's a very him word,' says Chris.

We arrive in Boston and head for a radio station, Kiss 108.

'Another tour, another radio station,' says Neil.

'Another Power CHR station,' says Chris.

' . . . that's not playing our records,' says Neil.

Jack Satter is here to meet us. 'Hey! How ya doin'!' He greets Pennie. 'You were in the show!'

'No,' she says.

'Oh.'

At the reception Jack Satter has a whispered argument. The only sentence I hear is 'I think *someone* knows they were coming.'

The DJ, when he appears, is called Dale Gorman. 'Are you doing radio interviews in every town?' he asks. 'They're tough. I don't do good interviews at all.'

'We'll be the judge of that,' says Neil.

He asks about the show. 'Why pigs?' he says, then adds, 'I mean, why not pigs?'

'It's to do with greed, I think,' says Chris. 'I'm not sure.'

'We don't know what it's about,' says Neil. 'We have to read the reviews to find out.'

He has a phone-in competition. 'What number caller should I take for these tickets?' he asks.

'Thirteen,' says Chris immediately. 'We stay in all these hotels and they don't have a thirteenth floor and it spooks me out.'

The DJ, it turns out, is quite a fan. He tells them how big Dusty Springfield's 'In Private' was on this station. Neil mentions that they offered it for the soundtrack of *Pretty Woman*: 'they didn't want to know'.

★

In the car Arma and Jack Satter discuss, in America record business-speak, tactics with '. . . Streets . . .'.

'We'll push it when the club base gets real solid,' says Satter. 'It's really starting to heat up. I think the mistake we made with "So Hard" is that we went with it straight out of the box. Some stations are a bit iffy about ". . . Streets . . ." and might be more likely to play it if it didn't have the Frankie Valli segment in. They're all rocket scientists . . .'

We arrive at the venue and there is immediately a sponsorship row. Outside the theatre, above 'Pet Shop Boys', is 'Reebok'. Inside there are huge Reebok banners.

'They've got to come down,' says Chris.

'It's ridiculous,' says Neil.

They walk out, both to be seen to be walking out and because they want to get something to eat.

'Shall we do a *Hard Day's Night*,' wonders Neil, 'and not go back until eight o'clock?'

The Orpheum Theater dressing-room, Boston, 6.30 p.m. Arma presents one further time the deal that has been sketched out for returning to play concerts in the summer.

'The smallest would be eight to ten thousand. We'd start in mid-August, go for six weeks.'

'How long would you have off?' Chris asks Neil.

'About two months,' says Neil.

'I need a four-week holiday,' says Chris.

'We can get the guarantee,' Arma continues, 'to average about $50,000 a night. That would cover our overheads, and everything you sell in percentages and overheads goes into profit.' He tries to bolster confidence. 'These promoters wouldn't be doing it unless they thought they were going into percentages. If we did moderately well you'd gross about $4 million and your costs would be $1.5 million.'

'Our concern,' says Neil, 'is that the equation might not work. Our experience is that one thing doesn't necessarily lead to another.'

'You came into the market with promoters who didn't really believe in you,' Arma points out, 'and didn't advertise you much. The word of mouth on the tour is incredible. You can tell from the merchandising sales that these are real fans.'

'These are our fans,' Chris agrees. 'We're worried about how well it can cross over to a mass market.'

'This is a major risk for the promoter,' says Arma, '$100,000 to $150,000 a night, and not one of them has asked, "Is there going to be a hit single?"'

'But will they go and see it?' Chris wonders.

Arma naturally says yes. 'With this show they'll go and see it twice, and bring five of their friends the second time. There's no one out there this summer with this sort of show . . . '

Chris gets to the crucial point. 'So we can't lose any money?'

'No,' says Arma.

'When do we need to decide?' asks Neil.

'In a week or two. While they're hot about it.'

'We should decide,' Neil says. 'So we don't piss about, and we get it in our heads.'

Arma presses on. 'I'm planning this with no single success. If we get lucky with the single then we're talking a different ballgame ... *multiples*. We could maybe do a pay-per-view – that's maybe $150,000 to $200,000.'

'We could maybe think about sponsorship ...' says Chris. He sounds serious and you can see Arma looking pleased. 'Because it seems we get sponsored anyway. Pepsi is always on our ticket.' This is a constant gripe. After all their efforts to avoid sponsorship, time and time again they find that the venue or the promoter has done a deal with a sponsor which surreptitiously associates them with the sponsor – usually by the sponsor's name appearing on the concert tickets or in the concert hall.

'We could get Reebok,' says Neil, for the return tour.

'We've just taken their banners down,' mutters Chris.

'They're vaguely English,' says Neil.

'They're South African,' says Arma.

'They're not?' splutters Neil.

'Just joking,' says Arma, alarmed. 'My opinion is that if you've got this huge thing running it'd be a mistake to pack it into boxes and not capitalize on it ... It's not a strenuous situation.'

'Strenuous enough, I think,' says Neil. 'Who's got a copy of this plan?'

'Ivan ... Richard ... Jill ...'

'Great,' says Neil. He turns to Chris. 'I think we should do it really. What do you think, Chris? Really.'

'I'd like to do it if it's successful, and I'd hate to do it if it's not. But I don't know if it's going to be . . . '

Arma has been inspecting the arriving crowds. 'A good audience,' he says. 'A lot of leather.'

'These are our new fans: the rockers,' says Chris.

They discuss strategy. Neil is unhappy that they are being promoted – unsuccessfully – at CHR radio.

'We should concentrate on alternative radio,' suggests Chris. 'CHR is over for us. We're too left field. We're underground.'

'We're underground,' Neil half agrees, 'in an overground way.'

'We're an underground car park,' follows on Chris.

'Parking an expensive car,' says Neil.

They bitch some more about EMI.

'I'm ready to drop a small bomb,' Arma promises.

'A *big* bomb,' Chris instructs.

'I found out today Richard Marx moved off. Now's our time to strike, whilst they're reeling over that. So I'm thinking of dropping that bomb tomorrow – if they don't break this record we want the greatest hits on another label.' He pauses, maybe even a little shocked at what their presence has led him to suggest. 'Shall I do that?'

'Yes,' mutters Chris.

'I think you should write them a provocative letter,' suggests Neil, 'summing up what's happened on the tour. I feel that when you write something down it focuses people. I vaguely think EMI haven't noticed . . . '

'I'll call Sal up tomorrow, say, "The band's not happy . . . " ' '

'Poor Sal,' says Neil.

'Say we've got no confidence . . . '

'Do you think it's worth talking to Sal?' Neil asks.

'Maybe I'll talk to Charles.'

'You should say, "We've got all this happening – how come we can't sell any records?" ' '

Chris sighs. 'You don't realize what an effort it is to do this show, do you, Arma?'

The opening music starts.

'This is where the crowd thinks, what on earth's going on? We're in for a difficult hour . . . '

★

Halftime:

Neil: 'I think your leather trousers are better than mine.'

Chris: 'Let's face it – the first half's dreary.'

Neil: 'It's like Chekhov.'

Chris: 'What shall we change when we come back? "This Must Be the Place"? It's dreary, but I suppose we can't change it. "It's a Sin" is a hit. "Losing My Mind"?' He shakes his head. 'I quite like masturbating. But *that* won't be happening in Blackpool.'

Neil: 'It's been called the Gay "Wall". I wonder why. It's got more heterosexual sex in it. And nobody calls it the Lesbian "Wall".' Neil looks for his T-shirt for the second half, but it is missing. 'Wardrobe have gone to pieces,' he says to me. 'Please note that.'

Alan: 'I'll sue.'

During the finale Craig is wearing a sheet of paper stuck to his back saying 'kick me'.

'This is our final night of our first-ever tour of America and it's been a fantastic experience for us,' Neil tells the audience.

'Well, that was it, then,' he says in the dressing-room, 'our first American tour.'

'So it's goodbye to the United States,' says Chris, 'and hello to Canada, sin capital of the world.'

'Of which,' Neil chips in, 'it's been said, "It's very clean . . . " '

'Why doesn't Michael Jackson put some money into us?' Chris wonders. 'Why didn't he come? Why didn't Madonna bring him? She's seething with jealousy in Malibu – Jean Paul Gaultier had already phoned her up. He did say, "It's the first time I've seen a rock show that is a real show . . . " and he did do the clothes for Madonna.'

Arma is still miffed about the Royalton. 'I'm never staying there again.'

'Chris,' says Neil, 'that place, it's falling apart.'

'I think we should go back to the Westbury,' Arma suggests.

'It's too stuffy,' says Chris.

'Chris, I *like* luxury and space,' says Neil.

'Me and Neil,' Arma tells Chris, 'have something in common. We like down pillows . . . '

Chris thinks of the return to America. 'We've got to think of new merchandise.'

'Wings rucksacks,' suggests Lynne.

'A wings T-shirt with actual wings coming out of the back,' suggests Neil.

'Little pigs to hang up in the car window like dice,' says Chris.

'Models of us,' says Neil. 'We should do a deal with TOYS'R'US.'

'BOYS'R'US,' sniggers Chris.

'You' – Neil gestures towards Arma and Chris – 'both like spending OPM. Other People's Money.'

They have some celebratory end-of-American-tour champagne.

'You know,' says Chris, 'I don't even like champagne. I've gone right off it.'

They sign autographs. Chris inscribes on one tour programme 'it was pure theatre, darling'.

'Can I take a picture of you?' a fan asks Neil.

'It's always best just to take it,' he advises. 'One's instinct is always to say no.'

Once the demand for autographs has been satisfied they scramble on board the bus. 'Do you know,' says Chris, 'we give value for money?'

We pass the mall.

'It's got Hermès,' says Neil approvingly. 'It's talking my language.'

'I don't really know what I'm about at the moment,' bemoans Chris. 'I haven't got an image fix.'

'You've got an identity crisis,' laughs Neil. 'You're unnerving the dancers.'

Arma has made that EMI phone call. 'I told Jack we may have some big problem. We're not feeling it on all levels. We need to talk.'

'We had too much success here early on,' says Chris.

'By the time *Actually* came out,' says Neil, 'we were like Abba. Now we're like the rad-est group ever.'

'That means we can make rad-er records,' celebrates Chris. 'I'm sick of making commercial records. I'd like to make a record that was really off the wall.'

'I'm going to have a Martini,' says Arma. 'We call it Loud Mouth Soup.' He proposes a toast. 'I was worried,' he confesses, 'about using pre-recorded music.'

They jump down his throat.

'We don't use any,' Chris huffs.

'You use tapes,' says Arma.

'We don't use tapes!' exclaims Neil.

'It's all live,' says Chris.

'It's machines playing live,' Neil explains once more.

'You think that's tape?' Chris asks Arma.

'People don't see the distinction,' sighs Neil.

'We could make life easier putting things on tape,' Chris points out. But, of course, that is rarely a Pet Shop Boys priority.

They move on to Ivan, giving him a hard time for earning too much money, and having too nice a hotel room.

'One of the reasons we left Tom,' warns Chris, 'is that he always had a better room than us. So remember that.' He's talking about Tom Watkins, their old manager.

'That's simply not true,' Neil laughs.

'He always had large rooms,' Chris insists, 'and we had piddly little ones.'

Arma asks about Tom. 'I've heard so much about him, but the more I hear, the more I like him.'

'Tom was fun,' says Neil, 'but he pissed off everyone in America.'

'And you still sold more records,' laughs Arma, 'with him than with me.'

The *Daily News* review has been hidden from them, but it finally turns up, and they pass it round the dinner table.

'It's a *good* review!' says Neil. ' "If you had to pick one word for this show – besides brilliant – it would be busy." ' He reads on. 'This is brilliant, "this does for pop music what Sunday in the Park with George does for theatre..." '

'Killed it,' mutters Chris.

'This guy,' says Neil, 'makes the point that it set out to intimidate the audience. It does, the first half.'

Chris reads it. 'This is much better than *The New York Times*! "The entire Met Opera on Ecstasy"! This is fantastic!'

They talk once more about the summer tour. Ivan is all for it. 'I think you could make an absolute fortune with the possibility of even more money than you could imagine.'

'You'd get a bonus,' Chris tells him. 'Whereas if we lose money we expect you to pay...' He laughs. 'As long as we make a lot of money I don't care.'

Arma is still peeved about the Royalton. 'I had thirty rooms booked there and I cancelled them because they woke me up at 7.00 a.m. both mornings. Fuck 'em. They lost about thirty thousand dollars. I'm going to the Westbury. I like chintzes. I like down pillows.'

'Don't slag off the beds,' says Chris. 'They're the most comfortable.'

'I didn't slag off the *bed*,' Arma points out, with commendable pedantry.

'You slagged off the pillows,' says Chris.

He asks about accommodation in Paris.

'Why aren't we staying in the Crillon?'

'You can't put the dancers there!' says Neil.

'Never mind the dancers!' says Chris. 'They can stay in the Holiday Inn.'

A clubbing trip is being planned.

'I refuse to go,' says Neil. 'I'm knackered.'

'You've got to come,' Chris insists. 'If you don't come they won't believe who we are . . . '

Some fans in the lobby have been removed.

'The fans have been thrown out,' chuckles Chris.

'For not being attractive enough,' says Neil.

'It's going to be a top night tonight,' Chris predicts.

We turn up at the first club. 'We're not paying to get in,' says Chris. There are negotiations. 'Do we want a big scene?' Chris asks. 'People ousted from their tables?'

There is some horrible local band playing, or so we assume. Then I recognize a song, then the next song too. We have wandered into a Pop Will Eat Itself concert.

'We hate them,' says Neil. 'They hate us.'

'Are they any good?' Chris asks.

'Chris,' chides Neil, for even entertaining the possibility, 'they're a footnote to a footnote.'

We go to another club – Ramrod's – but we can't get in: tonight's door policy is strictly leather.

Some girls who have somehow joined in our limousine entourage sing 'Feelings' and '911 is a Joke'. They ask whether we have ID.

'Of course we don't,' scoffs Chris. 'We're all over fifty.'

We go to Chapps. A man comes up and harasses Neil. Neil later describes him as a maniac.

It's been a funny night. We are drunk and tired.

'I don't always deliver,' rambles Chris. 'You know the twenty per cent of first-class mail that doesn't get delivered the next day. I'm that twenty per cent.'

We pass a shop whose window proclaims 'more beds than you've ever dreamed of'. Chris stares at it. It's ridiculous.

'Do you dream of beds when you're asleep?' he scoffs.

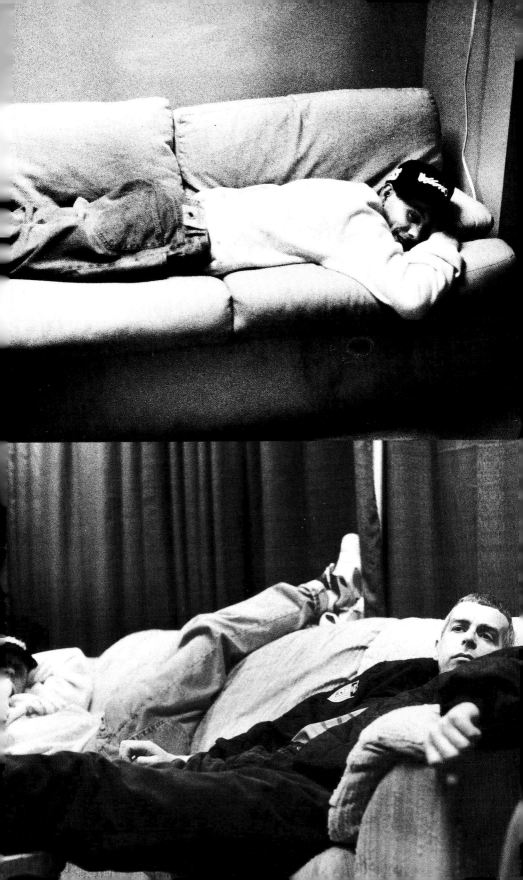

EXIT

Friday, 12 April

An airport panic. Chris has packed his passport in his check-in luggage and it must be retrieved.

'A good hassle,' declares Neil. 'It's a nice goodbye to America for the book.'

'Yes,' says Chris, 'we don't leave . . . '

Chris is now convinced he's left his passport by the side of his bed at the Royalton. Neil says it will be in his bag.

'Have you heard,' Chris asks, reading a newspaper while we wait, 'Michael Jackson's idea for a film? Busby Berkeley meets *Star Wars*. It's the same idea as everything he does.'

'He's a one-idea person,' says Neil. 'If I was Michael Jackson I would play a drug addict homosexual who's had a sex change.'

Chris's bag is produced. He rummages. 'It's not in the Filofax . . . ' he announces, there being an air of triumph accompanying this non-discovery. He rummages some more. Scowls. 'Oh,' he sighs sadly, 'it is here. How annoying. Drat.' He is going to Canada after all. He retires to eat some consolation pepperoni pizza. Then he hits upon a new tack. At the desk he instructs Ivan to inquire about the make of plane. 'Is it an airbus? I still might not come.'

It's a 727.

'That's OK,' Chris admits. 'They're over-powered, and they're tried and tested.'

Toronto airport:

'Oh,' chirps Chris. 'It's great to be in Canada!'

'Shall we have a glass of champagne to celebrate our arrival in one of the world's most exciting cities, Toronto?' suggests Neil. 'My kind of city: Oslo, Dortmund, Toronto. "I like Toronto – it's clean," says Neil Tennant, thirty-six.'

We board the bus.

'Actually,' says Neil, 'Toronto is just like England. It's just like England Part 2. Canada must be the only country that's got a logo. And it's got a tune. Every little bit helps. It's so insecure it needs to be marketed. The immigration guy said, "I think we've got a better understanding of British bands here." It was the first "I've got a chip on my shoulder about America" comment. The first of many . . . '

He puts a pre-release tape of Massive Attack's LP into the cassette player. 'Unfinished Sympathy'.

'I don't know why we don't make records like this,' says Neil.

'*You* keep wanting to make "It's a Sin" all the time,' answers Chris.

'This,' responds Neil, 'is the one that sounds like Fauré's Requiem. If you set Fauré's Requiem to a drumbeat we could have a big hit.'

Chris sighs. 'But we'd never be able to work out the chords.' Pause. 'I suppose we could get Richard Coles in.' One day, several years ago, the Pet Shop Boys were at BBC's Maida Vale studios recording a version of Kurt Weill's 'What Keeps Mankind Alive' for a radio special on *The Threepenny Opera*. They couldn't work out quite how to play it and so Richard Coles – previously one of the Communards, but working next door with Sandie Shaw – popped in and played it for them.

Chris spots a street name. 'Islington Avenue! I can't wait to get back to Islington.' He is thinking of Arsenal. 'What day is the FA Cup Final? I hope it's our day off. We could reschedule it otherwise.' He probably means the day off, not the Cup Final.

'Chris,' says Neil, 'why are you pretending to be interested in football?'

Neil changes the tape. 'I want to listen to my favourite song.' It's REM's 'Losing My Religion'. Along with the beginning he sings the Mamas and the Papas' 'California Dreamin'': 'all the leaves are brown . . . '

'Band and crew meal tomorrow,' Ivan tells them.

'Somewhere cheap and cheerful,' instructs Chris.

'No,' provokes Ivan. 'Really expensive.'

'For the *crew*?' says Chris, deliberately offensive. 'We want "a fun ambience".'

'The crew are really sophisticated,' Neil points out. 'The most sophisticated eater on this tour is the soundman.'

REM drone on to lesser matters. 'I've never understood the appeal of sounding crap,' says Neil, silencing them.

And we chat. Grammar comes up, and I mention that when writing for *Details* magazine in America the word 'like' is forbidden in those cases where 'such as' would be the pedantically correct term.

'That would be us,' says Neil approvingly. 'If we were Madonna it would have been *As Though I was a Virgin*. Our new album: *As Though It were a Prayer*.'

And then back to Canada.

'A very nice place,' says Neil. 'With politics. It's mega-concerned about equality. They have a sort of moral chip on their shoulder.'

We pass the Canadian National tower.

'There it is,' says Neil. 'The world's tallest building. The world's largest chip on your shoulder. Now they're building something in Chicago. They can't let the Canadians get away with having the world's tallest structure. It's taking the piss. It's like Sweden having it.'

We pull up.

'No doubt you'll have a better room than me,' grumps Neil to Chris. 'You always do.'

'No I don't,' says Chris, flabbergasted that Neil is trying to turn this traditional argument around.

'You do,' insists Neil.

'I'll only say two words: Radio City,' announces Chris triumphantly. '*You* had a piano and a suite; *I* only had a toilet annexe.'

They head off on room inspection.

'I'll see you in ten minutes,' Chris promises Neil, 'for a row.'

The hotel:

'I've got an idea for the next tour,' says Neil. 'It's all theatrical, but *it makes sense*! It's the logical next step.'

'I don't think we should do another tour,' says Chris, 'until we've got a hit album. Also, I think we've got to piss about with the next album. We've got to record it, then scrap it and re-record it, and really piss about . . .' He thinks. 'We should nick that slogan from Richard Branson and take the piss out of it: "A Rembrandt doesn't come on sale very often . . ." ' This is what Richard Branson said when committing huge sums to signing Janet Jackson to Virgin records.

'The idea of Janet Jackson being a Rembrandt . . .' sighs Neil.

'It's so preposterous,' Chris concurs.

They have just read that Michael Jackson's new LP will be called *Dangerous*.

'He should do a good album this time,' says Chris.

'I think he'll make an album that's more black,' says Neil, 'because the whole of *Bad* is like a Coke commercial.'

Silence.

'I'd hate to be Michael Jackson,' says Chris quietly.

'Imagine waking up as Michael Jackson,' says Ivan.

'What a terrible Kafkaesque . . .' says Neil, never quite finding his sentence's final word.

'He's circumcised,' Chris says. They know someone who stood next to him in the toilet and noticed.

Saturday, 13 April

Chris and I go to Neil's room, where he is on the telephone to Reuters.

'... I don't really think that what we do is limited to gays. We don't regard ourselves as Erasure. It's not why we do what we do ... I don't agree with the concept of role models. How can anyone say they're a role model? ... People aren't stupid, you know. People know. I would never set myself up as a role model. I have no interest in it ... People get out of this music, depending on who they are or what they are, what they want out of it. I mean, some people want to dance to it, some people's mothers like it ...'

The interviewer clearly mentions a song on *Behaviour*, 'Nervously'.

'People pick up that, but it's not meant to be explicit. The "nervous boy" in the song is me ... I personally think we have a very honest approach to all of this, but in the media it's very difficult to discuss. There are plenty of people who live totally deceitful lives, and the Pet Shop Boys could never be accused of living totally deceitful lives.'

I can hear the journalist's voice: 'I think it's important you live an honest life.'

'You don't think we're honest?' Neil is a little indignant, and a little surprised. 'I think we are totally honest.'

They discuss the TV film about the history of gay disco which Jon Savage made for *Out on Tuesday* in 1988.

'It's a rather large subject. Then, the predominant style of music, dominated by Stock Aitken Waterman, was gay-derived pop music. I think I said on the programme Rick Astley's music was gay disco music, and it was. It was the predominant style in eighties pop, from Frankie Goes To Hollywood to Jason Donovan: it was gay-derived. There are people who would argue that all disco is gay dominated, and I think they're probably right. Then, in the sixties, it was dominated by gay managers ...'

There is another, unheard question.

'I don't want to talk about it,' says Neil firmly. 'We are musicians, not politicians. I think the people you're talking about are politicians, not musicians.

Who else are you talking about in Hollywood? In television? The reason you can sit here and ask me is because we're *not* dishonest. We are in a unique position because we're not dishonest people. We are the only people in the whole world you can talk about like this.'

'Put the phone down,' Chris advises.

'You and I could both name ten or so Hollywood stars,' continues Neil down the phone, 'but you couldn't discuss it with them because they're dishonest.'

The conversation drifts onwards.

'I find it patronizing that to get over messages about AIDS you get a load of second-rate cover versions . . .'

Red Hot and Blue, one presumes.

'We never do those things, because we like to think that what we do is totally unique. We don't want to be linked with that . . . I know it's a very unfashionable view, but I don't think pop music exists to service causes. It exists to make good music . . . What's the car industry's response to AIDS? Why don't they make a car and give the money to AIDS? Why don't Hollywood make a film and give some of the money to AIDS? Why don't Reuters give twenty per cent of their money to AIDS?'

But pop stars . . .

'People want to be regarded as great humanitarian figures. I don't want to be a great humanitarian figure. I'd rather be presented as mean and spiteful than a great humanitarian figure.'

The next question is clearly about his relationship with Chris.

'We speak; we're friendly. That's how we started. We're not lovers if that's what you mean . . . Somehow I get more attention because I'm the singer, but I don't think he minds that because he doesn't crave attention . . .'

Neil mentions his love of Noël Coward. The interviewer doesn't know who he means.

'He died in 1971. '73, sorry. No, I never met Noël Coward, to my eternal regret . . . It's these very British kind of silly songs. It's music that's from a tradition, kind of different and similar to what we do.'

He is asked whether he is politically active at all.

'Yes. I vote. I don't belong to a political party. I always vote for the Labour Party in Britain. I personally think the most effective way of change happening is through the ballot box, and I don't think pop stars have much effect on that. I think the only thing that pop stars have had a major effect on is to persuade people to take lots of drugs. They have had some effect on the green movement, but the green movement existed before Sting. The other effect is maybe on clothes: in training shoes. Pop is fashion, you know. That's the whole point of it. If pop stars are involved in the environment and it becomes fashion, in a few years there'll be groups going "screw the environment" because it's a fashion and it's a pendulum. And it should be. Pop stars used to persuade people to take drugs, then they persuaded them not to, now in England they try to persuade them to take drugs again. It's a fashion.'

Neil smiles at the next question. 'No,' he says, 'I couldn't sum up a single message from our songs.' Chris laughs. 'I think we put out a complex set of messages, some of which are contradictory. It's how you don't have a single message, and how difficult it is to live life in a complex, difficult world.'

The interviewer mentions shopping.

'Even shopping,' says Neil, 'isn't easy.'

'That was exhausting,' says Neil once he has finally put down the phone.

'Did he ask you if we were sexy?' Chris asks.

'No one ever asks that,' says Neil.

A French interviewer is next. As he asks his questions Chris browses through a copy of *Classic CD*. Neil reels off the usual.

'We always thought that people in America liked things that were different, and I think we've been proved right.'

Why, asks the Frenchman, are you starting the European leg of the tour in Paris?

'It had to start somewhere,' mutters Chris.

'I don't know why,' Neil chips in. 'It seemed like a sensible place.'

In England, says the Frenchman, you are big stars, but in France you are . . .

'. . . little stars,' completes Chris.

'I think maybe the words are too English, and the words too complicated,' says Neil. 'A lot of music crosses language barriers because the words are so simple.'

'Actually,' says Chris, 'I think the French are very lucky that we're going there at all.'

The interviewer asks about the computer technology.

'We couldn't be bothered getting musicians together,' says Chris, 'and it's easier using technology, and musicians are a miserable bunch – they're

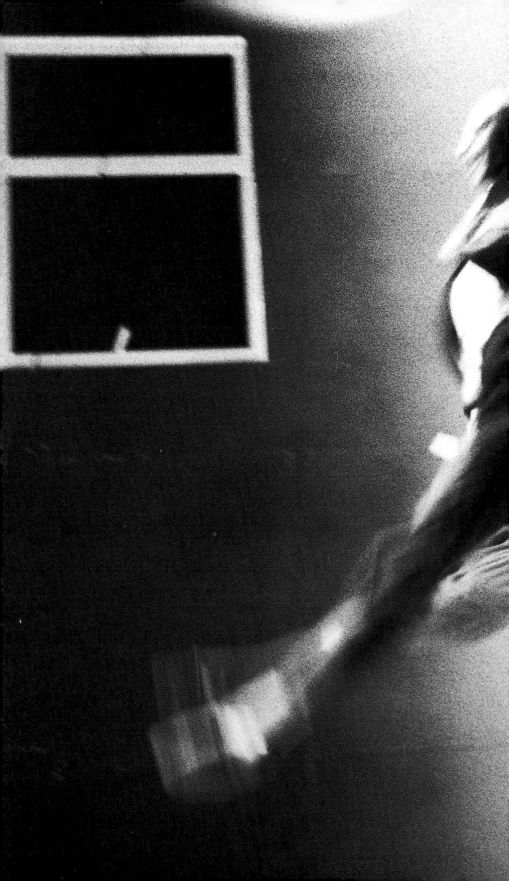

temperamental, they get colds, they don't travel well. Then they all start getting off with girls. You don't get that with machines.'

Neil bides his time, then reinforces this with the more considered explanation he has been relating throughout the tour.

Do you think, asks the now rather bemused Frenchman, that dance music is liberation?

'Of what?' asks Chris. 'Of the soul? I don't understand the question.'

'Do you find dance music liberating?' says Neil, rather beginning to take the interviewer's side.

'Yeah,' says Chris. 'I dance my rocks off.' Slowly he expands. 'I don't really like saying I like dance music any more because here it's all swingbeat, but in Britain it's not just the music, it's a whole fashion thing ... a way of life. In America it's just something to do on Friday and Saturday night.' He looks at Neil. 'I think Neil goes to clubs for different reasons. I go to dance.'

Neil laughs, and looks a little embarrassed. 'I go to drink and talk.'

They are canvassed about Hammer, still 'MC' at the time.

'To be honest,' begins Neil, 'I don't really like rap music in the main. It doesn't really express anything for me. I like music – no matter what type – that makes you feel something, and MC Hammer's music sounds, at best, like an advertising jingle. Which is fair enough, because he's about money, isn't he? He's maximizing his financial capability at the moment.'

Chris eats a Caesar salad with spaghetti as the interview continues, just throwing in the occasional aside. Neil is asked about new projects.

'I think our next project,' interrupts Chris, his mouth full, 'will be a Gap advert.'

'I think we're bringing out a greatest hits LP,' says Neil.

'It'll have fewer tracks in France,' mutters Chris.

'In France it'll be an EP,' says Neil. 'In fact it won't come out...'

So, battles on the interviewer, video is important for you?

'It depends,' says Neil. 'Sometimes it's something you just have to do, but given that you have to do it, you put quite a lot into them. I think "Being Boring" is the best video we've made, that and "Domino Dancing". It's very beautiful and it captures the feeling of the songs. We like beautiful things. In America they only show it on the Playboy channel. They can't deal with male nudity – they find it too shocking. They can deal with female nudity.'

Will they make another movie?

'I don't think so,' says Neil. 'Did you see the other one?'

The Frenchman leaves. The mood is strange – rather flighty and carefree.

'I don't think we should do any more press. I hate doing interviews,' says Chris. 'I don't know whether we should do any ever again.'

'I'm beginning to wonder if we should give up,' says Neil.

'We could still make records,' says Chris.

'I mean retiring from the business,' says Neil. 'I kind of think we've had it, and I couldn't face going down the slippery slope. I think it would be wonderful to go out with a number-one greatest hits.'

'That was the Pet Shop Boys,' says Chris.

'I think we've got a real real fundamental problem at the moment,' says Neil, 'which is going to be difficult to deal with, and I really really seriously feel it, and I think it's based on our personae.'

'That's why I think we should disappear,' says Chris.

'It doesn't make any difference,' says Neil despondently, 'because when we come back we're still us.'

'We could stop being in our videos,' Chris suggests.

'That's a good idea,' Neil agrees.

'I'm bored by us,' says Chris.

'I'm totally bored by us,' Neil agrees. 'Watching those interviews on video yesterday totally sickened me. I'm totally bored by us ... actually, I think one thing we do well is press interviews. I think the press interviews we've had this time have been really good. I think the interviews you've done are really good. I just don't know that we should be seen in the TV age. And I think the solution for us is to be like the "Being Boring" video, where we're in it but not in it.' Pause. 'I feel at the moment we should chuck it in.' Another pause. 'I think we're seen as so negative. We've had the same personae for so many years that it's not surprising the public have got bored of it. I don't blame them, because I'm bored of it too.'

'I'm worried about coming back to America,' says Chris.

'I'm just so aware people are bored with us,' says Neil. 'It's impossible not to be aware of that.'

There is a very long pause.

'The Bee Gees kept on going, didn't they?' says Chris.

Neil is not moved by this. 'Do you really want to be the Bee Gees?'

'Yeah,' says Chris.

'No,' objects Neil.

'They seem quite good,' Chris insists. 'They occasionally have hits. They're quite talented.'

'Well,' sighs Neil, 'there you are . . .'

The dressing-room looks, Chris reckons, 'like the Conservative Party Conference'. They joke about the earlier interviews.

'Your interview technique,' Neil says to Chris, 'is now to say something really vile, in a voice that doesn't sound ironic.'

Chris smiles. 'When are we going on?' he asks Ivan.

'8.15.'

'Can't we go on sooner?' he complains.

But they can't. There is a delay. Robbie has sent out for a replacement lighting generator. Neil says he's 'shattered' and requests some Wow! They chat about drugs. 'No one prints my quote about drugs,' moans Neil (meaning what he told Reuters about how pop's most successful advocacy has been not for noble causes but for the encouragement of drug-taking), 'and it's probably the only outrageous thing I say. They probably think, oh, he's trying to impress me.'

Long pause.

'Montreal's going to be half empty,' says Neil, 'and we can't curtain it off.'

'I blame the public,' says Chris, 'and I'm going to say so.'

'They can't account for it,' says Neil. 'They are utterly bewildered.'

Alan asks about tonight's dinner. 'Is this dinner paid for by the promoter?'

'No,' says Neil, 'it is going to be paid for by Neil and Chris out of the generosity of our hearts.'

'It's only cheap,' Chris reassures him.

'Chris and I,' says Neil, 'are going to go round and say patronizing things like "thank you, you've been *marvellous* . . ." Prince Charles said to Curiosity Killed the Cat, "It's these synthesizer things that are ruining music." We'd have said, "No, you're wrong." '

Chris shows off his yellow Montana T-shirt. 'It only cost $145,' he laughs. 'I only bought three.' Even Neil is shocked. 'I got a yellow one and a black one and a blue one,' Chris laughs. 'It's got a good neck on it.'

Ivan informs them of a merchandise scandal – on the sly the merchandisers have started printing the T-shirt on Screen Stars, not Hanes T-shirts.

'If we come back in the summer they won't have the deal any more,' promises Neil.

'Ivan, tell them they've all got to be destroyed,' says Chris. 'It's taking the piss.'

'They should sell them for less,' Neil suggests.

'They're not trustworthy,' grumps Chris.

'No one in the T-shirt business is trustworthy,' Neil points out.

'They're not invited to our dinner either,' says Chris.

'Certainly not,' agrees Neil. 'Tomorrow night,' he instructs Ivan, 'we're selling them for five dollars less.'

'And,' says Neil, 'we're not taking less money.'

Halftime:

Neil: 'I'm sorry – it's the best show of the tour.'

Chris: 'They're a smashing bunch of people.'

Neil: 'I'm going to say, "I love you".'

Then they talk about schooldays . . .

Neil: 'At school I was called a poof.'

Chris: 'It's because you weren't very good at football.'

Neil: 'No, so I had to get richer than them.'

Chris: 'You should buy the school.'

Neil: 'I still may, and close it down.'

They discuss this book.

Neil: 'We could call it *Out and about in America with the Pet Shop Boys*.'

Before they reappear in their leather gear Chris says to Neil, 'Why don't you go out with a banana down them, just for a laugh. I think that it might make the difference.'

Somehow this rather fits tonight's mood. So he does.

I meet up with him losing it after the first few numbers in the dressing tent backstage. 'It was incredibly unnerving,' he says. 'I could feel it slipping. If I do it again I'll have to have it gaffa-taped.'

His closing speech is 'This is the first time we've ever played in Canada and it's a night we won't forget for a very long time. Thank you.' Then, as promised, 'We love you.'

'Well,' says Dainton backstage, 'you rocked Canada!'

'We've got to do it again tomorrow,' says Chris.

'I think it was the best crowd of the tour,' says Neil.

Chris has had an idea. 'We could call our greatest hits *Farewell*.'

'Or,' suggests Neil, '*Split*. Then we'll have to say, "Oh, no, we're not splitting – it's just the title." '

'*Pet Shop Boys Go Their Own Ways*,' suggests Chris.

'*Pet Shop Boys Hate Each Other*,' laughs Neil. 'Or *Semi-detached*. *Pet Shop Boys Semi-detached*.'

'That's good,' says Chris, 'but will they get it in America?'

'No,' sighs Neil. 'That's why we're calling it *Long Live Rock'n'Roll*.'

'*It's Alright*,' says Chris. '*Twenty-three Quite Good Songs by the Pet Shop Boys*.'

A pause.

'I couldn't really give up this life,' Neil admits. 'The adulation . . .'

'You've got too much love to give,' says Chris.

'Yes,' Neil agrees. 'All these smiling faces. And a couple of grumpy bastards in the front row. Some people are embarrassed to like it. They *quite* like it. It's rather like us if we went.'

Ivan comes in with the latest on the merchandise situation. The man in charge of merchandise is squirming. 'He'll do anything,' Ivan chuckles. 'He's flying up tomorrow to apologize.'

There is a drink organized by Canadian EMI to present a gold disc. They meet some fans.

'We've decided we're overexposed – we're retiring at the end of the tour,' Chris tells one rather distressed fan.

A man walks up to Neil. It is Ian Balfour, the author of 'Revolutions per Minute or The Pet Shop Boys Forever'. Their conversation is interrupted by EMI's attempt at a presentation. Neil and Chris had already said they didn't want any fuss and when they are rather flamboyantly announced Chris walks away.

'I love you, Chris,' says another fan to him as he leaves.

'I'm sorry,' he says. 'We've got to go.'

Chris says he wants to go back to the hotel.

'I thought you were going straight out,' says Neil.

'I'm not going straight anywhere,' he says.

Sunday, 14 April

In the morning Ivan tells them that last night's festivities – an extended drinking binge in a Toronto nightclub for the entire touring party – cost them six thousand dollars. 'A complete waste of money,' says Chris.

They're still smarting about the presentation. 'It's embarrassing getting a gold disc,' says Neil. 'It's like getting a disc for not selling any records.'

The conversation drifts on to the subject of Chris's parents and the way they have still not mentioned the events of *The Tonight Show.*

'It's literally unbelievable,' says Neil. 'You could be a serial killer and they'd visit you in prison and they simply wouldn't mention it. I quite admire that. It's that there's nothing to profit from saying anything.'

Ivan reports on the merchandisers. As penance for sneakily substituting inferior-quality T-shirts they've been forced to reduce their prices tonight while maintaining the Pet Shop Boys' cut. 'You don't ever substitute,' fumes Ivan. 'It's the oldest trick in the book. It's kids' stuff and when people do that kind of shit you've got to hurt them and let them know, and the way to hurt these people is financially.'

Arma runs down negotiations with EMI. The feeling is that they are still not too committed to '... Streets...' In America it is very difficult to have a big hit without full record company commitment.

'I think we should ask why, in terms of EMI, the Pet Shop Boys toured America,' says Neil. 'It was EMI's idea in the first place.'

'You're really just a hit away from multi-platinum status,' Arma consoles them.

Arma asks about doing some promotion tomorrow in Montreal.

'I'm doing nothing,' says Chris. 'We decided yesterday that we should never do televised interviews because we're too old and ugly.'

Arma persists, saying they should at least visit *Musique Plus*, a music TV station.

'I'm just not into it any more,' says Chris. 'It's easier to say no. Just Say No: that's my slogan for the tour.'

This is the culmination of Chris's fury at not being consulted about such interviews until after it's too late to cancel them.

'What tends to happen,' agrees Neil, 'is that they come to me and I say, "Ask Chris", and they don't.'

'Because they're afraid of Chris,' points out Arma.

'But it's not my fault if they're afraid of Chris,' says Neil.

'This is the least interviews I've seen on a tour,' Arma declares, changing tack.

'Exactly,' says Chris. 'It's a holiday. Pet Shop Boys on holiday.'

'Ten minutes!' says Alan.

'It's fifteen,' proclaims Neil.

'It's when we decide,' mutters Chris.

I wander round during the first half of the performance. J.J. is playing in half-light totally backstage. I look at the set-list at his feet. After the final encore, 'Your Funny Uncle', he has written, as though it were the next song, 'Hotel Bar'.

Halftime:

'Where is Wiggsy?' frets Chris. 'He's slipping up.' Pause. 'Where are my goggles?' he barks.

' "Where are my goggles?" he barked,' says Neil.

'Banana! You've forgotten the banana!' says Chris.

'I'm not having it tonight,' says Neil.

They go back out. During 'So Hard' – as, spookily, Chris had predicted three weeks before – some fans get out umbrellas to match those on-stage.

Backstage:

Neil sings 'Mad Dogs and Englishmen' then fiddles with his contact lenses.

'You shouldn't have bad eyesight,' suggests Chris.

'Chris, I can't help being disabled,' Neil replies.

'Well,' says Chris, 'why did you choose to have bad eyesight?'

'It was a means of drawing attention to myself,' Neil bluffs back. 'Sub-consciously I wanted to be different.'

Chris noticed for the first time tonight how Neil takes his applause before lying down at the end.

'I didn't know you did a bow,' he teases. 'It's really funny.'

'My nauseating bow,' mutters Neil.

Steve, the man from EMI, runs through tomorrow's interviews with Chris. He wishes he hadn't.

'I'm not doing any promotion,' says Chris.

'Oh,' he says. 'Ivan said it wouldn't be a problem.'

'Well, he didn't ask me,' says Chris.

A few minutes later I hear Neil saying, 'Chris gets pissed because no one ever asks him anything. It kind of happens a lot and it drives me mad . . .'

When he leaves Steve cheerily pipes, 'See you tomorrow!'

'They're not seeing me tomorrow,' says Chris.

Chris signs some autographs out back, while Neil is still dawdling inside.

'Where's Neil?' someone asks.

'He's hiding,' says Chris. 'He just can't face the fans. He's become very insular.'

A few seconds later, of course, Neil joins him.

In the bus, driving overnight to Montreal, Chris puts on *This is Spinal Tap*.

'The minute my back is turned!' exclaims Neil, who has banned it from being watched on the tour so far, on the grounds that it is a little too close to the truth and a bad influence. After the first ten minutes, and several exclamations that 'it's just like us', he says, 'I find it too depressing.'

After a while Arma appears from the back of the bus and asks, a little too anxiously, 'Have they fired the manager yet?' Then Spinal Tap start talking about their planned musical and Chris hoots, 'Neil! Neil!'

'That depressed me as usual,' says Neil once it's over.

'Why?' asks Chris.

'I don't like the way they go down the pan,' he answers. 'And all that "Boston isn't a big college town" is just . . . too depressing.' And too much, he doesn't say, like the keep-smiling rationalizations that the American record industry has been tossing their way for the last month. He pours some champagne – 'this is rock'n'roll, right?' – then, once he's sure Arma isn't in earshot, says, 'I was embarrassed watching it in front of Arma. There's a classic manager bit . . .'

They quiz Ivan about whether he committed them to these interviews tomorrow.

'Did you tell him it'd be all right?' asks Neil.

'I said, "Write it down on a piece of paper," ' says Ivan. 'It's not my place to confirm it.'

'They need to be taught a lesson once and for all,' says Chris.

Now they are caught in the classic bind which the record company relies upon. If they don't do the interviews they won't just not promote themselves, it will have a negative effect. They will be the Pet Shop Boys, the group who cancelled an interview they had agreed to.

'I think it was a good idea to do *Musique Plus*,' suggests Neil.

'It was a good idea,' agrees Chris, 'but I'm not doing anything now.'

'It's cutting off your nose to spite your face,' Neil objects.

'Yeah,' accepts Chris, 'but they've got to learn. The first I hear about something can't be when he says he'll meet us at the airport to go do it.'

Toronto Star, *15 April, 'Neil Tennant, the talent behind Pet Shop Boys.':*
Now, there goes a clever boy. And there goes another who's not clever at all . . . The British techno-poppers showed that Tennant is the talent behind all the studio artistry, while Lowe is simply the 's' that makes Pet Shop Boys plural rather than singular . . . Lowe appeared as little more than a roadie who had forgotten to exit the stage . . . Lowe acted more as prop than performer . . . At all times Tennant displayed a strong sense of showmanship, which he must have picked up during his days as a rock journalist . . . But one shouldn't take Lowe or the Pet Shop Boys too seriously, as they surely don't take themselves.

Monday, 15 April

True to his word, Chris refuses to do the scheduled interviews. But the Pet Shop Boys are expected, and tonight's show is far from sold out, so Neil sets out to do them alone, with Arma, Pennie and myself in tow. In the car the talk is of whether Chris will even turn up for the performance. Arma telephones Dainton and instructs him 'to make sure Chris gets to the gig'.

'Do we have an official reason why Chris isn't here?' wonders Neil.

'He was feeling faint,' says Arma with the authority of someone who has to paper over far bigger cracks than this.

'He has taken a drug overdose,' suggests Neil, 'and he's having his stomach pumped.'

'He has an intense dislike for French Canadians,' laughs Arma. 'Somehow,' he adds, 'I've got a funny feeling you've played this movie out before.'

'I've never appeared on TV alone before,' Neil points out.

'Except for the Johnny Carson show,' Pennie chips in.

'Yes,' he concedes, 'but we *started* out together.'

'The video goes to MTV today,' he tells Neil.

'We find out how much they hate it,' says Neil.

We pull up outside *Musique Plus*.

'Oooh,' says Neil, '*nous sommes arrivés.*'

He is seated in the middle of the open-plan office and interviewed live.

'Actually,' he tells Canada, 'he's not feeling well . . . but he'll be there. He's a professional.' And then the usual 'it's so far removed from a rock show it's not even in the same ball park . . . ' and so on. They play the 'Being Boring' video.

'Arma,' says Neil, 'this video is too good not to be played on MTV.' They have refused it because of the nudity. 'This is such a good record – it's a classic.'

We head off. 'All the tickets we sell over what we've sold now,' Neil tells Arma, 'I want Chris's share of the money, because I've sold them.'

'I doubt Chris will see it that way,' suggests Arma.

'Arma,' teases Neil, 'as our manager you've got to tell him.'

We arrive at dance music radio station CKMF and Neil is interviewed: 'A

Their 1991 Performances.
Lundi 15 avril · 19h30
Auditorium de Verdu
Sièges réservés en vente à l'auditor
à tous les Ticketron ou au 288-

lot of our songs aren't about the happiest things, they're about real life; falling in love; being disappointed; making money; suffering; working; being happy . . . in Japan we had a review that said we were being boring and we thought it was funny and I just started singing "we were never being boring" . . . We set out to do something totally different, and it's kind of nerve-racking: they might hate it. But it's been a thrilling and moving experience . . . '

Afterwards Arma fills Neil in on the latest EMI discussions. 'They were asking me if they can schedule the greatest hits. I said you can't schedule it until there's a hit attached to it.'

'That's good,' says Neil.

Chris is waiting when we arrive at the ice-rink where the concert will be. He doesn't like Montreal. Everyone speaking in French. 'I speak in the broadest northern accent possible,' he says.

Some Coca-Cola banners are up in the hall. There is the usual fuss.

'Arma! Have you seen this?' says Chris.

Arma winces. 'I think this is probably the same as Radio City – someone presents all their shows.'

'It looks as though the Pet Shop Boys are endorsing Coca-Cola,' Pennie accurately points out.

'Every major promoter is tied in with a sponsor,' demurs Arma.

'It doesn't seem right that we don't get any money,' says Chris.

'This is the dodgy new bollocks,' huffs Neil.

'We should also get a sponsor,' Arma once more suggests, hopefully.

'Or not get a sponsor,' adds Chris. 'We always said we wouldn't.'

'I doubt whether your fans know about your position on it,' hints Arma.

'Have you read the interview?' laughs Neil, picking up a new interview in the *Montreal Mirror* in which he explicitly trashes and condemns corporate sponsorship in pop music.

'You *didn't?*' says Arma, laughing. He reads it. In it Neil says, 'We have no sponsorship. Our show is total content. When someone comes to our show, they enter our universe. If you go to see Michael Jackson, you don't enter Michael Jackson's universe. You enter Pepsi-Cola's universe. It's like entering a big office-building. I think it's destroying music.'

'Well,' sighs Arma, 'so much for corporate sponsorship.' He thinks a moment longer. 'Have you ever contradicted yourself in this career?'

'Most of what we do is a contradiction,' says Neil. 'We've never been consistent.'

Chris is annoyed enough to go to Ivan. He wants an announcement disassociating the Pet Shop Boys from Coca-Cola. Ivan says it's not possible – the promoter is never going to risk annoying Coca-Cola like that for just one concert.

'They're slippery bastards,' Chris fumes. 'I'm never going to drink Coca-Cola again.' His fury rises. 'Or Pepsi.'

In the venue restaurant the conversation winds on and, just as they are deep within a bizarre discussion about whether it would be good for Madonna to be a man for a year, Robbie appears.

'They're coming in really slowly,' he says, 'not that there's many to come in.'

'Robbie! There's no need to put it like that!' says Neil. Then he turns to Chris and says, 'Let's not do the whole show tonight.'

'We could miss "My October Symphony",' Chris suggests.

'I like that,' agrees Neil. 'Why not cut the whole first half?'

They pretend to decide that from now on they will cut the show according to how full the hall is. Ticket sales are worst in northern Italy. 'In Milan,' sighs Neil, 'they'll get two and a half songs.'

They return to the dressing-room – a drab ice hockey changing-room with benches and an old sofa.

'I want you to take a good look at this place,' says Arma, 'because you'll never have to play somewhere like this again.'

I ask them some questions:

Two years ago you said that for pop stars to succeed in America what they do has to reduce into one very simple message. Where does that leave you now?

Neil: 'I think they have reduced us to a very simple message, which is "they're kinda sick".'

Why do you want to be successful in America?

Neil: 'Why do you want to be successful anywhere? It personally irritates me when a record that ought to be popular isn't. I don't like someone thinking that someone else's record is better than mine.'

Chris: 'I don't mind us not being successful; it's other people's success I don't like. It really annoys me when loads of people like the same record, and the record is crap.'

Were you dreading this tour before it began?

Chris: 'I can't remember what I thought. (*Looks at Neil.*) Was I looking forward to it or what? I probably wasn't. I was probably dragging my feet, complaining to everyone, asking why we were doing it.'

Neil: 'I was apprehensive, but then I'm apprehensive about most things.'

Do you think your reviews here have been accurate?

Chris: 'I don't know.'

Neil: 'Well, I don't think it would be possible for us to carry off the show if we were a one hundred per cent totally charisma-free zone.'

Why do you think you're not more popular in America?

Chris: 'We're too good.'

Halftime:

'I'm quite enjoying this for some reason,' muses Neil. 'They're very happy and positive.'

It is now that Neil chooses to express unhappiness about their leather outfits.

'You've got better trousers than me,' he sulks, 'and better boots.'

'You chose them,' says Chris.

'No,' replies Neil, 'I *agreed* to them. It's different.'

'You should put a banana and two lemons down your trousers,' suggests Chris, 'to make it more realistic.'

Just before they go Chris is arguing, 'I don't like Q. I don't like CDs. It's too consumerist.'

Neil stares at him, and, for a moment, is too affronted to speak. '*Chris!*' he scolds, 'that is *my* spiel.'

At the end of the stage Neil says, '*Nous sommes les Pet Shop Boys.*'

'He'll do anything for a few extra sales,' says Chris afterwards. He refuses Dainton's offer of champagne. 'I don't want champagne any more. I want beer. It's a working man's drink.'

In the bus Chris whispers, '*Nous sommes les Pet Shop Boys.*'

'All right, that's enough from you, Lowe,' says Neil.

We eat at Zen, a Chinese restaurant beneath our hotel.

'I'd like to congratulate someone,' says Chris, raising his glass. 'Me.'

'I'd like to congratulate me,' challenges Neil, 'for delivering five hundred people.' Five hundred more people bought tickets today.

Then they have a real toast.

'Tap into America!' says Neil.

'You're the only people I know,' says Ivan, 'who can call a tour successful when it's lost $500,000.'

Chris accuses Neil of using an American accent when singing 'Your Funny Uncle' on-stage. Neil disputes this.

'I'm just saying what you did,' insists Chris.

'I didn't.'

'I wouldn't have said you did, if you didn't.'

'You thought I did, but I didn't.'

'You did.'

And so on.

Gazette, *Montreal, 16 April, 'Pet Shop Boys camp out':*

Ludicrous . . . Tennant's vocals, which he would readily admit are close to Al Stewart's, were deadpan and dead on . . . Hey, show biz, it's their lives, babe.

Epilogue, April 1993

The Pet Shop Boys' 1991 tour continued successfully throughout Europe (in Britain they finally relented and added 'Being Boring' as an encore), but 'Where the Streets Have No Name . . . ' was not an American hit and they did not return to play the sheds. Their greatest hits album was released in November 1991, eventually titled *Discography*. It was preceded by a single, 'DJ Culture', based around the idea Neil had come up with in America.

After the tour Dave Cicero, the Scottish artist signed to their Spaghetti record label, began releasing records with varying degrees of success. 'Love is Everywhere', one of the songs they listened to in the back of the limousine in Miami, reached the top 20. They also signed Trevor and Mark as a rap duo to Spaghetti under the name Iggnorance, and the two of them recorded an album for release in 1993. They continued to use Sylvia on various projects, though in 1992 she found greater temporary fame duetting with actor Jimmy Nail on his number-one hit single 'Ain't No Doubt'. Likewise Katie Puckrik began to get the attention she desired as one of the hosts on the ramshackle British Friday night TV show *The Word*.

Jay Leno took over the reins of *The Tonight Show* as planned, though, following worries about the working practices and success of his new regime, Helen Kushnick was subsequently ousted from the show. Sal Licata is no longer head of EMI.

Naturally the Pet Shop Boys themselves did not split up and, at the time of writing, are completing a new album for release in the autumn of 1993. They have no plans to tour again in the near future.

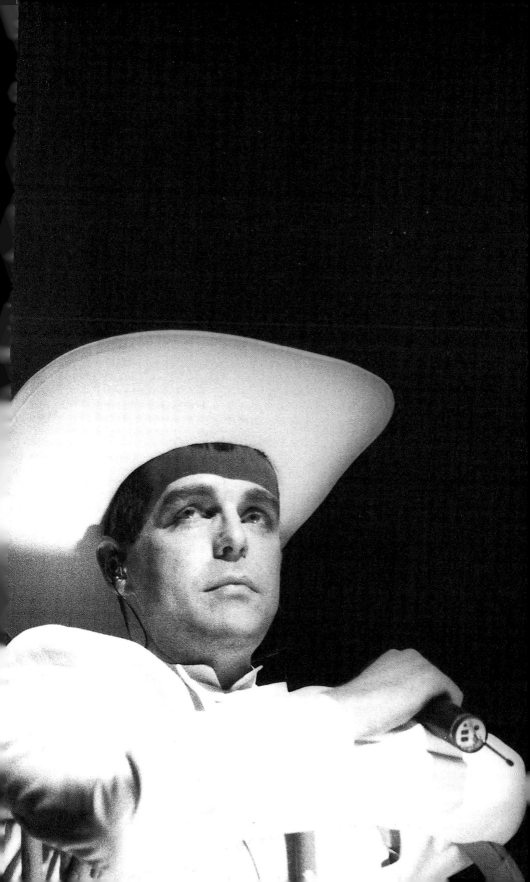

List of Photographs

Pages 154–5: Pet Shop Boys on the bus from Chicago to Detroit; Neil writes and Chris eats cornflakes.

Pages 158–9: Scenes from 'How Can You Expect To Be Taken Seriously?'; Pet Shop Boys are confronted by pigs and images of themselves.

Page 161: Neil asleep on the tour bus.

Page 165: Neil, assisted by Alan and Chris backstage at the Bender Arena, Washington, dressing as schoolboys.

Pages 166–7 (top): A scene from 'Where The Streets Have No Name'; Trevor, Katie and Craig dance.

Pages 166–7 (bottom): Some dancer's cups.

Pages 170–71: Stopping *en route* between Washington and New York. Left to right: Chris, the author, Ivan, Neil and Arma.

Page 176 (top): Neil giving Trevor a singing lesson backstage at Radio City Music Hall

Page 176 (bottom): Neil and Liza Minnelli backstage.

Pages 182–3: Chris signing autographs on the limousine bonnet outside the artists' entrance at Radio City Music Hall.

Page 186: A scene from 'Where The Streets Have No Name'; Neil and Chris (wearing a bowler hat in the background) amidst a Las Vegas production.

Page 191 (top): Mark and Trevor as angels outside Radio City Music Hall.

Page 191 (bottom): Mark, Trevor, Neil, Chris and Suki on the streets of New York.

Pages 194–5: A scene from 'West End Girls'; Chris drunkenly kicks out.

Pages 200–201: Scenes from 'Jealousy'; Pet Shop Boys are crushed to death by giant Oscars.

Pages 208–9: Chris, horizontal in Miami, Houston, Minneapolis and Toronto.

Page 210: A scene from 'Always On My Mind'; Neil plays guitar.

Pages 218–19: A scene from 'Always On My Mind'; the dancers dance.

Page 224: Pet Shop Boys receiving a gold disc backstage at the Varsity Arena, Toronto.

Page 226: A scene from 'Always On My Mind'; Chris plays keyboards.

Pages 232–3: Chris backstage at the Verdun Arena, Montreal, with a concert poster.

Page 235: Neil introduces Chris to the audience.

Pages 236–7: A scene from 'Your Funny Uncle'; Neil sings the final lines while Chris sleeps.

Page 241 (top): Neil says goodnight.

Page 241 (bottom): Chris and a truck.

Pages 242–3: Pet Shop Boys with the fans from Mobile outside the Saenger Theater, New Orleans.

Page 244: Pet Shop Boys.

Back cover: The Orpheum Theater, Minneapolis.